MVSI

"YORK MUSIC"

The story of a city's music
from 1304 to 1896

by:

James Merryweather

cartoons:
Ingrid Johnson

SESSIONS BOOK TRUST
The Ebor Press, York, England
1988

"YORK MUSIC"

Text & Design © James Merryweather, 1988.

Cartoons © Ingrid Johnson, 1988

Printed from the Author's camera ready artwork by
William Sessions Limited,
The Ebor Press, York, England.

ISBN 1 85072 034 7

DEDICATED

To the memory of Percy Scholes and all my good friends, the
late waites, who currently languish in the archives of this
great city of York.

ACKNOWLEDGEMENTS

Many, many people have helped with this project and I would like to thank them all for their contributions. Firstly there were the local archivists: Mrs Mary Thallon and Mrs Rita Freedman, (York City Archives) Chris Webb, (The Borthwick Institute for Historical Research) John Clarke and staff, (York City Reference Library) the staff of York Minster Library, and Pat Cullum who found Thomas le Wayte. Then there were the professional historians specialising in York's past, Dr Charles Kightly and Dr Eileen White, who helped this rank amateur get his facts straight. Next, the photographers, John Clarke, (another one) Steve Thompson, (not the melodeon player - this could become very confusing) Simon Laycock, and Dick Hunter, as well as Jef and myself, and their models: Jef Maytom, Helen Hale, Harry Vallack, Martyn Craft, Roy Grant, Nev Hobson, and The York Waits. Thanks to Ingrid Johnson for her witty cartoons in which historical detail is dead right, especially in the clothing. Financial support was generously given by Mrs Ruth Shannon and the Pilgrims of St Oswald, Fulford thanks to the encouragement of Roy Grant. The Commodore 64 computer and Easy Script made the typing and text revision a doddle and typesetting possible, if a little primitive. Moral support was always available from Peter and Sylvia Hogarth and Corita Myerscough, all engaged in similar York researches, as well as Mr Timothy Taylor (brewer of Keighley) in association with Nev of the John Bull, and Tom and Brenda of the Brown Cow. Finally, thanks to dear Rebecca Nicholson for patiently putting up with constant reports on and draft readings of "the obsession" before running away to Ecuador while I get on with the laborious typesetting.

CONTENTS

FOREWORD

The Early Music Movement in Britain has led the world over the last twenty years - and in that time we have seen many colourful manifestations of this extraordinary revival. In my experience nothing has been more colourful than the sight of five virile young men blasting their way down the medieval high street of Middleham Town (North Yorkshire) playing their bizarre collection of instruments, dressed in their unforgettable costumes, with their unique black titfers on their heads - The York Waits, in all their glory, entertaining the populace, young and old, serious and zany.

I have been completely taken in by these characters - a chapter of forgotten history come to life? Now one of their number with pretensions to scholarship presents us with the background documentation of nearly 1,000 years of Waits history, searching out in a most learned way much arcane knowledge of this curious phenomenon. Actually I suspect that the real aim of all this erudition is to justify historically that essential talent of wind-players, the downing of well-brewed ale. Some things don't change much - and this 1,000 years' history proves it.

And it's a jolly good read too - I recommend this book to you.

Anthony Rooley

PREFACE

In 1836 an act of parliament put an end to centuries of tradition. Some of the trimmings of civic life were to be curtailed and a restyled, more down-to-earth style of local government was to be encouraged. Throughout the nation a number of council offices were abolished for ever, including the musicians responsible to their Mayors for civic entertainment and ceremony: **The City Waites.**

Today, as we speed towards the twenty-first century, the waites are all but forgotten. Their name lingers in the memory of older citizens but very few could tell you of their doings. It is now over one hundred and fifty years since they played for their Mayors, and we have little left but local archives in which to seek the lives and personalities of the thousands of musicians who served their communities over some six hundred years.

There have been a few brief histories of the waites nationally and locally but none has attempted to paint a picture of the men, their music, and their life-styles. Most have been content to transcribe the ancient records and discuss the mundane details of guild laws and wages. In York the archival evidence is plentiful and I have had the good fortune to "get to know" our waites with some intimacy, although the imagination is one of the most important tools of my trade. (That is not to say that any of what follows is fictitious). After summer evening sojourns in the libraries and document stores of York I have spent many whimsical hours in the churches and parishes of my long-deceased friends, soaking up the atmosphere of their environments of centuries past. This (in the words of Jane Austen) "partial, prejudiced, and ignorant historian" discovered with pleasure the, literally hair-raising experience of, after hours of laborious attention to stained and faded documents in virtually illegible archaic handwriting, finding those few words which bring the story alive. I vividly recall the day that I reluctantly called for aid from Chris Webb of the Borthwick Institute when puzzling over the will of John Harper who passed on in 1539. Chris gently deciphered, to my amazed delight: "....I will and bequeath a noys of pipes called shawmes...." It was that sort of experience which turned me from one who hated and failed in history at school into an altogether different creature. To my unfortunate companion, who was obliged to listen to my droning on about each latest discovery, this work became known as "the obsession", and no-one could be happier to see it finished and in print than she.

It is to be hoped that some of the imagined waites' personalities may be made available to the reader through this book. As you will see I have made use of my friends and the camera to present scenarios from York's musical past. I presume that no-one will think these are original photographs. As you no doubt appreciate, photographs from these early periods are extremely rare and difficult to reproduce.

I would have most liked to offer my story about the waites to Percy Scholes, born in 1877 at Headingly, Leeds, author of the acclaimed Oxford Companion to Music. He died a ripe eighty one years old in 1958 so I would be somewhat overoptimistic to pursue that desire for long. He saw the possibility of discovering more about the waites in 1934 and said so thus:

It is surely, not a small thing, that for four centuries or more every English town of size (and probably every Scottish one, too) possessed its own little municipal orchestra. The history of the English waits is still somewhat obscure, and will remain so until a few thoughtful and patient musicians in different parts of England set to work to dig into their local archives and tell us what they find. Anything concerning the waits of any period should certainly interest us.

Scholes's desire that more people should take an interest in the waites has hardly been met by a flood of literature. I regret that I am too late to be able to show Percy my contribution to the realisation of his dream. It is quite evident from his own writings that he was a man of enthusiasm and good humour who would have enjoyed getting to know the York waites ("Naturally", I hear you say, "he was a Yorkshireman"). Nevertheless this work is for him and, perhaps in the future, I shall be able to follow it with sequels for as many of the British towns with recorded waites as time will allow.

It is, perhaps important at this early point to clarify my spelling of the main word in this text. The form: "Wait" I reserve for the modern early music band THE YORK WAITS, although it will turn up occasionally among the many different spellings that occur when I quote from original documents.

In my text I will use the common, archaic forms: **"Waite"** and **"Waites"** throughout.

The terms "freedom" and "free", used frequently in the text, refer to an essential trading requirement in York. No man could trade in the city without first becoming a freeman by one of three means: he could undergo a full seven year apprenticeship; he could claim freedom by patrimony; (that is, his father was a freeman) or he could be ordered to take his freedom by the Lord Mayor and council because the city had need of his skills. The date of a musician's appearance on the roll of freemen is frequently the first we hear of him and as such is of great interest. It is also of use in determining family pedigrees, for father and son relationships are given.

James Merryweather
York, 13th March 1988

BRUSSELS, 1614

YORK, 1983

INTRODUCTION

"The appropriation in modern days of the name waits by wretched street players and singers at Christmastide is unfortunate, as it has thrown contempt on the memory of a worthy institution. It seems curious that in England, where the cultivation of music has been advancing for many years, a good thing has been allowed to decline and finally die out, while hordes of incapable foreigners are encouraged".

FA Hadland, 1915[17]

Ask most people today if they have heard of "the waites" and if their reply is affirmative, they will almost certainly associate them with Christmas and music. Until the beginning of this century small groups of musicians would perform in the wintry streets by lamplight, playing seasonal tunes or singing and playing Christmas carols. Even today people like to perform their carols after the same fashion and many traditional greetings card designs feature the waites singing picturesquely in Victorian snow scenes.

A glossary of 1859 (Surtees Society vol 35) gives its definition thus:

WAITES-Musicians who still parade the towns in the North of England at Christmas Tide. At Newcastle one of the towers was called The Waits Tower. Their musical abilities at the present time are not of the most striking description, but formerly they were deemed worthy enough to assist the choristers in the (York) Minster.

Waites were the municipal bandsmen of the days before the city councils were reformed by act of Parliament in 1836 (The Municipal Corporations Reform Act). Until then most towns and cities in Britain supported their own musicians but they went along with several other traditional offices abolished at that time. People missed the waites, especially at Christmas, when they would have played in the streets as they performed their night watch duties. Small groups of instrumentalists and singers got together to reinstate the tradition of carolling at Christmas. In the late 1830s they were often the redundant town or city waites, but plenty of incompetents jumped on to the vacant "band-wagon" gaining the art a thoroughly bad reputation which is complained of by Hadland[17] and reflected by Punch, the magazine which first appeared in the early 1840s. Mr Punch lampooned "the Christmas waits" for one hundred years, from 1843 until Roland Emett (the author's favourite cartoonist: see "The Last Tram") had a last dig at them in December 1943. Generally, it seems that they were an annual nuisance, playing abominably and annnoying everybody:

SURE SYMPTOMS OF CHRISTMAS, no. 13:

Because the waits wake me up at night, paying me the discordant compliment of playing opposite my window longer than anyone else's.   (Dec. 1853)

WAITS AND MEASURES

What a pity it is that London should be so far behind Birmingham, where that energetic Chief of Police, Major Bond has commenced a crusade against the Waits, in the following grimly ascetic:

"CAUTION.-Numerous complaints are made of the disorderly conduct of youths who go around the suburbs of the town during the nights of 24th and 31st December, 'begging' under the new pretence of saying 'A Merry Christmas' and 'A Happy New Year'. All persons found so offending will be apprehended by the Police, and charged with being disorderly characters".

There! Birmingham is blessed with its own BOND. London is free-worse luck! Failing police protection against these Christmas nocturnal disturbers, might we not adopt the irate suggestion of a misanthropic old Brute, who sends us the following recipe:-"Keep in your bedroom a garden-engine, its reservoir filled with ice-cold water, of which give any Wait full measure".

(Jan. 1877)

THE WAITS!

A MERRY Christmas! Ah! no doubt;
  And those within *seem* vastly merry.
Meanwhile, 'tis precious cold without!
  Chilled fingers, nose-tips like the cherry,
They find, who're trying the experiment,
Are scarce conducive to much merriment.

Music hath charms! Of course, of course!
  But when the instruments all jangle,
When this seems cracked, and that sounds hoarse,
  And tune and time are in a tangle.
Soothing the savage breast—or warming—
Seems quite beyond its powers of charming.

Whew! what a wind! Leader, play up!
  Let's give 'em something brisk and rousing:
Perhaps they'll ask us in to sup,
  Or share awhile their gay carousing.
Something with less of shake and run in it!
This wait-ing game has little fun in it.

How they are going it inside!
  There's little RANDOLPH toasting SOLLY!
Their very shadows swell with pride,
  Their laughter rings out bright and jolly.
How different it *might* have been!—
Tip 'em "*The Wearing of the Green!*"

If that won't fetch 'em, nothing will;
  And if we can but play together.—
Well, well, we'll try it. Tune up, BILL'
  An outside berth in this cold weather
Suits none of us. Let's hope the fates
Won't keep us waiting long as Waits!

THE WAITS.

Punch, 26th Dec. 1885

Mr Punch was unable to resist every aspect of that obvious pun in the last line above, and annually used its possibilities to make satirical comment:

CHRISTMAS WAITS

Mr Disraeli waiting for something to turn up.
The farmers waiting for protection.
The railway shareholders waiting for a dividend.
Naval veterans waiting for promotion.
Everybody waiting for the good time coming.
THE HEAVIEST WAIT OF ALL.-Ninepence for a pound weight of Butcher's Meat!
(Dec. 1849)

and still he hated the waits:

SIX "WAITY REASONS"
(for suppressing Street Musicians.)

BECAUSE carols are never entirely satisfactory when suggestive of frequent visits to a public house.
BECAUSE a trombone, a bassoon, and a concertina should be in time and tune to give due effect to a midnight rendering of the Mistletoe Bough.
BECAUSE "merry gentlemen" can never "sit at home at ease" with howling on the crescendo in the street outside.
BECAUSE an application for largesse at 1am is inappropriate and irritating.
BECAUSE the plea that "Christmas comes but once a year" is absolutely unnecessary.
Lastly, because Yuletide would be a long way "merrier" without them.
(Dec 1849)

**The Illustrated
London News
19th Dec, 1896**

Mr Punch's waits were frequently depicted as a small group of poor musicians (poor financially and/or musically) playing carols on cornet, trombone, clarinet, 'cello, or tuba, in an attempt to extract a few coppers from the well-warmed householder at Christmas time.

The Illustrated London News was also aware of the waits and a beautiful woodcut (see page 11) illustrates its opinion of them: two rival waits bands brawling, presumably to settle a territorial dispute.

These 19th and 20th century magazines depict the waits of relatively modern times, they who still just linger on the edge of living memory. Quite a few authors tell of the Bradford waits,[44] elected in 1829 by a magistrates' session at the Spotted House, a pub which still serves the community in Manningham Lane. Blind Sam Smith was given leave to form a company of waits and he enlisted three fellows who were also blind! The four minstrels tied themselves to a pole so that they could be led around town by a fifth, sighted man, their guide. In York there were four brave gentlemen who persisted as Christmas waits: Dick Whitehead and Harry Bramham, violins, with John Pottage and Isaac Oglesby, 'cellos. One wonders if they were as awful as Mr Punch's horrors? The text of TP Cooper's little book "The Christmas Waits and Minstrels of Byegone York" (1909)[9] implies that they were a popular local institution. Their final performance was in 1902 and perhaps their musical presence at Christmas was much missed by the residents of this city.

Having introduced the musicians who called themselves "waits" within living memory, it is necessary to discount them from the rest of this book. It is the waites of earlier times, for whom the "Christmas Waits" were merely a nostalgic replacement, whose history is to be related. The true waites originated in distant medieval times, and until 1836 the Lord Mayor

and corporation of York had maintained a band of city waites for at least
four hundred years. The city records occasionally minuted disciplinary
proceedings against the waites, and these amusing anecdotes describing their
misdemeanours have frequently been used as a basis for unjustly defamatory
characterisation of these, generally well-behaved professional musicians.
This story is an attempt, not only to discover the lives of a large number
of forgotten York personalities, but also to "put the record straight" with
regard to those who were, or were not, indicted of being "drunk in charge"
(of a musical instrument?).

The waites played the music for all civic ceremonies: mayor-making,
sheriffs' ridings, grand processions, banquets and dances, as well as
occasionally accompanying the choir at the Minster. At night they
perambulated the streets, keeping watch and playing to mark the hours.
The night watch was a relic of waites' original duties. In even earlier
times (13th-14th centuries) cities and dignified households employed
watchmen, "vigilators", to protect their sleeping occupants. These watchmen
frequently carried a horn (as does the Wakeman of Ripon today), or other
loud instrument to sound the alarm or to announce the changing of the watch,
and it is very probable that the musical part of their activity increased in
importance. The name "waite" may have been derived from the watchman's
association with the "wayte", "wayte-pipe", or shawm, the main instrument of
the waites before 1600. A similar term is still in use in Europe, now
applied to bagpipes, close relatives of the shawm: "gaite", "gaita", "gaida"
etc. It may also be a corruption of the Anglo-Saxon term "waician" which
apparently means "to watch".

Let us curtail this amateur etymological argument, for it seems to the
author that others who quote the derivation of the word have plagiarised
other amateur sources. Until a competent, modern philologist attends to the
word we will all have to decide for ourselves by reference to the vast array
of lexicons and encyclopaedias available.

In York sources the earliest spelling of the term, in 1434, was "wayte",[62] with contemporary variants "wate", "watte" and "waytte". By far the most common spelling, from the early 16th century right through until the 19th century was "waite", the "e" being dropped in more recent times (the "Christmas waits"). As stated in the preface this work will use the spelling "waite" for the waites of the past to avoid confusion with THE YORK WAITS, the early music group from modern York who have revived the band as it was in the 16th and 17th centuries.

The waites of York appear frequently in the city records and careful collation of entries in parish registers and indexes of wills with city council's records has enabled a detailed picture of York's musical life to be prepared. The York city archives contain great stores of written records which include almost complete collections of the council's minutes and the city chamberlains' (those responsible for civic spending) accounts. These were written by hand on vellum, now bound into magnificent volumes. Unfortunately they have suffered greatly from age, damp, (occasionally flood) and vermin. Even so, these accounts of York life, which include many tales of the waites, may be read and laboriously copied in pencil - the original authors produced sufficient inky blots and modern researchers may not further blemish these priceless pages. Some examples used to illustrate the text will give some idea how handwriting changed over the centuries and how the untrained eye (ie that of the author) might cope with deciphering it. The truth is that at first encounter he failed to recognise the writing as English! The information gained from wills, the rolls of freemen and many other less prolific sources enable family relationships to be worked out, musicians' instruments determined, and some missing links in the story to be replaced. Much of the piecing together of the story took place in quiet corners of York's better public houses (ref. acknowledgements) where attention to pencilled notes, accidentally soaked with Mr Timothy Taylor's splendid "Landlord" ale, were consulted with puzzled head-scratching followed by muted whoops of delight as the proverbial penny dropped, sometimes accompanied by stifled tears of triumphant realisation that another tenuous connection had been proven.

Copies of York wills on vellum, 1681

that of John Edwards, waite, is on the left.

THE INSTRUMENTS OF THE YORK WAITES

"In like sorte many Cittyes mantayne at publicke charge Musitians, vsing Sagbutts, Hoboyes, and such loude Instruments, which wee call the waytes of Cyttyes...."

Anon, 1617

The instrument with which waites are usually associated is the **shawm.** In the manner of many renaissance musical instruments the shawm came as a family whose sizes reflected human vocal ranges. The treble shawm was the ancestor of the modern double reed woodwind instrument the oboe, and the larger sizes (alto, tenor, and bass) may be considered the ancestors of the cor anglais and bassoon. The shawm had a conical bore, a long, often widely-flared bell and a large, coarse reed enabling it to produce the volume and stridency required for outdoor music. The shawm probably found its way across Europe to Britain with travelling musicians who had been influenced by its music in the Holy Land at the time of the crusades (12th-13th centuries). The first appearance of the shawm in York records may be in the roll of freemen for 1343[7] in the entry of William de Lyncoln, registered as a piper. "Piper" indicates not that he played bagpipes but woodwind instruments generally, the shawm probably being in his collection. Shawms were certainly the instruments of the York waites in the 16th century, to be superseded around 1585-90 by the more expressive, but no less powerful ensemble of cornett, saggbut, and curtal[26].

Soprano, Alto, & Tenor Shawms

Bass Shawm & Double Curtal

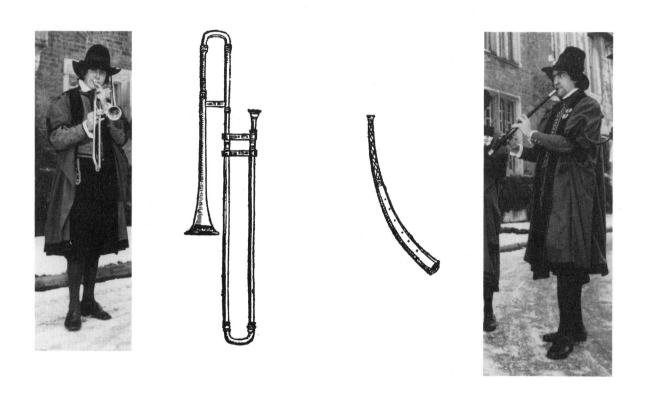

Saggbut & Cornett

The **curtal**, in York (1602) the double or bass curtal,[26] was effectively
the bass shawm bent in two for the convenience of the player and was the
evolutionary link between the bass shawm and the bassoon. It had a more
mellow sound than the bass shawm and saw long service with church choirs
all over Europe, doubling with the bass singers. Later this tradition was
continued by the bassoon or, in many English village churches by the
serpent.

The **saggbut**, as it was usually called in York,[26] "sackbut" in other parts
of the country, was the trombone, originally invented early in the 15th
century and it remains little changed today.

The **cornett** is now extinct. It was an instrument originating in the late
middle ages, probably as a cowhorn trumpet. Cows unfortunately do not supply
horns at predictable pitch and the cornett was manufactured to allow the
player to play in tune with others. It was carved in two halves from wood,
then the halves were glued together and tuned finger holes bored in it. The
whole instrument was covered with leather to seal its inevitable leaks. The
air column was sounded by the player blowing trumpet-style into the small
mouthpiece which he placed at the side of his mouth. This was to facilitate
the tight embouchure required of so small a mouthpiece.

The French writer on musical instruments, Mersenne, in 1636 likened the
cornett's sound to a shaft of sunlight breaking into the darkness when heard
with the voices of a cathedral choir. More often than not, today's players
make it sound more like a gale howling past a flying buttress!

The **bagpipe** was a popular European instrument yet, to date, only three
York references have been discovered. A "bagge pype"[58] was amongst the goods
of the guild of St Christopher and St George in 1533[58] and William Hill, the
waite, bequeathed his "best baggepipe" in his will of 1558.[24] A splendid
poem describes the hanging of John Bartendale, bagpiper, at York in 1634:[54]

Here is a piper apprehended,
Was found guilty and suspended.
Being led to fatal gallows,
Boys did say, "where is thy bellows?
Ever must thou cease thy tuning."
Answered he, "For all your cunning
You may fail in your prediction."
Which did happen without fiction;
For, cut down and quick interred,
Earth rejected what was buried.
Half alive or dead he rises;
Got a pardon next assises;
And in York continued blowing:
Yet a sense of goodness showing.

Smallpipes by Julian Goodacre, 1980s

John Bartendale was indicted of an unspecified felony at the castle and executed at York's Knavesmire (as was Dick Turpin). A manuscript (British Library Add. MS 33,595) containing fragments of York history, owned in 1655 by Richard Girdler (thought to have been the same Richard Girdler as the fourth son of John Girdler, waite 1623-66) states that:

"....he hunge three quarters of an houre, was cutt downe caste into a hole with others covered with earth and feelinge the weighte of earth upon him beganne to stirre was taken upp [by a member of the local Vavasour family, fortuitously riding by and puzzled by the wriggling grave] carried backe to the castle & reprieved at the assizes following".

**English Bagpipe by
Jonathan Swayne, 1980s**

It is interesting to observe that (at least, in the knowledge of the poet) Bartendale's pipes were bellows-blown, as are the Border, Northumbrian, and Irish pipes of today, and unlike most illustrated English bagpipes of the period which were mouth-blown. That is not to say that it is not possible that Bartendale played 17th century "cold pipes" some of which are still in playing condition today.

Medieval Harp

The **harp** was played in York by William de Burgh (1319),[7] John Bannyster (1558),[7] and Ambrose Burghe (1561).[8]

There are two curious references to pipes which the author has been unable, so far, to identify.[26,58] Both are in 1596 in respect of the retirement of the elderly waite John Clerke in which it would seem that he made "holling" or "holyn" pipes and was required to deliver them (perhaps an outstanding order) to the Lord Mayor or forfeit his pension. He was indeed paid three shillings upon their delivery but what were they? The only possible meaning given by the Oxford dictionary is holly. Perhaps Clerke was given to use holly timber, a pure white, close-grained hardwood, in the manufacture of flutes or recorders. A positive explanation would be most desirable.

As 1600 approximately marked the change from the shawm band to the cornett and saggbut ensemble, so 1700 also represented a time of change in the waites' instrumentation. The **oboe** is first mentioned in the will of Joseph Shaw in 1703.[24] He also owned a cornett and perhaps was responsible for introducing the former instrument to York music with the consequent demise of the latter. The Assembly Rooms accounts 1730-80 frequently mention the five waites, one of whom is to play the "hautboy", and in 1739 the waites played in the grand procession to mark the declaration of war against Spain. They played upon "Hautboys and bassoons", immediate descendants of the shawm and curtal, the characteristic loud band of the Georgian period.[15]

For outdoor ceremony the waites of York undoubtedly used their suitably noisy and weather-proof wind instruments, but many of them did own **violin, viol,** or **lute** and were probably proficient upon them.[24] The string instruments would have given nothing but trouble out of doors as any modern string player will know, but indoors, at dinners and dances, they would have come into their own, the fiddle being especially suitable as a solo dance accompaniment.

Oboe & Bassoon

In the years leading up to 1836 and the end of the city waites in England, the small band of three included Daniel Hardman who was a 'cellist.[50] The 'cello seems to be a most unsuitable instrument for a waite's duties and although, some illustrations depict waites with the 'cello, it seems that Hardman was also a player of an unspecified brass instrument. Enderby Jackson recorded that[25]:

At the latter end of the year 1833 Walker and Hardman's celebrated York brass band was inaugurated. It consisted of twenty-four players, and speedily achieved an excellent engagement reputation. The instruments used were cornopeans (keyed bugles), French horns, trumpets, trombones, and ophecleides (effectively bass cornopeans).

James Walker, trumpeter, and Daniel Hardman had founded Yorkshire's first brass band, a novel concept, for this was also one of the world's first bands of a musical revolution taking place in the early 19th century. What instrument our last York waite played is still a mystery. A crumb of evidence in a picture by TP Cooper[9] gives one to wonder if it was the ophicleide....but then one of his waites has a 'cello and another, tantalisingly, has his back to us....and then Hardman, who in 1896 was in his nineties,[25] would have been about the age of the boy talking to the 'cellist. While the hunt for the truth about Daniel Hardman continues so must this account.

Trumpets and **drums** were heard in York throughout the time that the waites were active, but not played by the waites at any time. Trumpeters and drummers (and in the 18th century, **french horn** players) were specially employed and liveried by the corporation. From the late 14th century to the present the ceremonial trumpet has always been a simple conical brass tube, curled back on itself twice, with a flared bell for amplification (like the natural trumpet, the early french horn was also valveless).

A full chronological list of instruments in York literature is given in
Appendix II.

Trumpets & Kettle Drums

THE MUSIC OF THE YORK WAITES

Paſt three fair Froſty Morn,
Good morrow my maſters all.

Mr Durden, ca 1700

There is little music that was certainly played by the waites in York but, with careful reference to popular English music which the waites might have used, a fair idea of their repertoire may be proposed. Before doing so it should be considered that these musicians were apprenticed professionals, probably very skilled in the musical styles required of full-time civic employees and, moreover, far from being the drunken incompetents some modern commentators would have us believe. From the 15th century virtually no popular tunes have come down to us and there are no York tunes whatsoever. In the 16th century many popular dance and ballad tunes appeared and spread throughout the country, orally or printed on broadsides, many of which have survived. One nationally popular ballad tune, "The Hunt Is Up" (said to have been a favourite of Henry VIII)[6] first appeared in about 1534 and was in common usage until 1666 and later. Fragments of the tune have been found in folk music in the 20th century.[56] It began life as a ground, a bass line upon which tunes were built. There are two sources of evidence for its having been known in York, perhaps used by the waites. John Thorne, the minster organist, 1541-1573, wrote three devotional poems, one of which was certainly a mimic of the ballad "The Hunt Is Up:"[1]

The hunt ys up,	The hunt is up,
The hunt ys up,	The hunt is up,
Loe! it is almost daye:	And it is well nigh day;
For Chryst our kyng	For Harry our King
Is cum a huntyng	Is gone hunting,
And browght his deare to staye.	To bring his deer to bay.

The 1578 ordinances of the York guild of musicians (appendix V) mentions the waites' duty to play "Huntsups", an indication that they may have used the tune. One could hire the waites to wake one up in the morning and this musical aubade was referred to as a "Huntsup". The popularity of the Huntsup is reflected by its numerous appearances in literary sources:

A suite of descants **"y^e Hunte Yis Uppe"** arranged for the English Bagpipe.

And every morn by dawning of the day,
   When Phoebus riseth with a blushing face,
Silvanus' chapel clerks shall chaunt a lay,
   And play thee hunts-up in thy resting place.

                                              Barnfield, 1594

"....we were early up, being rous'd from our sweet sleep by the Citty wayts, (Chester) whose absence we had rather desir'd, nott for the charge, but for our rest".

                                            Anon. 1634

Past Three O'clock,
   On a cold frosty Morning,
Past Three O'clock,
   Good morrow masters all.

                    Anon. 17th C (to the tune "The Waits")

Many of the popular tunes of the 16th and 17th centuries must have been known and played by the waites of York. "Sellenger's Round", "Packington's Pound", "Trenchmore", and even "Three Blind Mice" are quite likely to have been in their repertoire. The broadside ballad by William Elderton,[37] about a real-life archery contest which took place in York around 1594 has a metre which is irresistably suggestive of the most popular of all 16th century tunes, "Greensleeves":

As I came throw the Northe Countrye,
The fashions of the world to see
I sought for mery companie,
    To goe to the cittie of London:
And when to the cittie of Yorke I came,
I found good companie in the same,
Aswell disposed to every game,
    As if it had been at London.

Yorke, Yorke, for my monie,
 Of all the citties that ever I see,
For mery pastime and companie,
    Except the cittie of London.

It is felt in York that the last line of the refrain should truly read:
"Surpasseth the cittie of London"!

"Greensleeves"

YORK WAITS

In a Winters morning, long before the Dawning, e'er the Cock did crow, or Stars their light w'

dran, wak'd by a Hornpipe pretty play'd along York City, by th'help of ter nights Bottle Damon mad'u

Ditty, but having none of Apollo's Humours, take what follows, tho' y' God till mellows, a dull wheazy Fellow

Words any Cat gut Scraper, w' a Kit w'uld Paper, soon can set to Musick, but some Tunes to fit w' unforc'd easy

Rhyme good Sense and yet keep Time, wou'd Puse a Dryden, and make Sing Song Tom to Sweat

In a Winters night,
By Moon or Lanthorn light,
Through Hail Rain Frost or Snow,
Their rounds the Musick go,
Clad each in Frize or Blancket,
For either Heav'ns be thanked,
Link't with Wine a Quart,
Or ale a double Tankard,
Burglers Scudd away,
And Bar Guests dare not Stay,
Of Claret Snoring Sots,
Dream o're their Pipes and Pots,
Till their brisk help Mates wake 'em,
Hoping Musick will make 'em,
To fit by pleasant Cliff that plays the Rigadoon
For an Entry Virgins long,
Widdows to be New Strung,
By some good able Master,
  And well play'd upon

for the

FLUTES

Candles four in the Round,
Lead up the Jolly Round,
Whilst Cornet shrill i'th' middle,
Marches and merry Fiddle,
Curtel with deep hum hum,
Cries we come we come come,
And Theorbe loudly answers,
Thrum thrum thrum thrum,
But their Fingers frost nipt,
So many Notes are her Slipt,
As that you'd take Sometimes,
The Waits for the Minster Chimes,
Then Sirs to hear their Musick,
Wou'd make him Sick or you Sick,
And much more to hear a roopy Fidler call,
With Voice like her that cries,
Who Shrimps or Cockles buys,
Past three fair Frosty Morn,
  Good morrow my Masters all,

Around 1700 a Mr Durden published his broadside **"York Waits."** In his preamble to a performance of this ballad at the Musical Association's session in 1928 (the legendary Canon Galpin was among the performers on that day) Prof. JC Bridge suggested that the tune was "an old hornpipe to which some doggerel rhymes were fitted and it was sold as a broadside".[3] The learned professor's assignation of the term "doggerel" to Durden's text suggests that he had not read the words or wished to cover up the fact that their meaning was clear to him. Although the song innocently describes the waites on their morning watch, perambulating the city by the light of a lantern, naming their instruments (cornett, fiddle, curtal, theorbo, and kit) and even kindly mentions a dance tune, the "Rigadoon", there are cryptic references to matters erotic and the beautiful descriptions of contemporary York life are merely a clever vehicle to disguise the author's witty obscenities! (The reader is asked to discover the hidden meaning for him- or herself.... or to enjoy the poetry at its face value, according to taste).

The tune of the ballad is indeed a merry hornpipe, but whether or not it was a waites' tune is not known (although freqently alleged). Its style suggests that it is contemporary with the words, that is from the early eighteenth century.

An earlier song on the same topic is found as the dance "The Waits", perhaps a tune of the London Waites, published by John Playford (The Dancing Master, 3rd edition, 1657).[4] The words (in no original source associated with the tune) have survived as the familiar Christmas carol "Past three o'clock", which refers to the waites' duty of patrolling the night watch, by the late 17th century merely a Christmas tradition.

"The Waits"

The small collection of music in
the York Minster library[16] supplies
a few hints to waites' music,
though there is no direct evidence.
The waites sometimes supplied music
in the Minster and may have played
the accompaniment to sacred works
performed by the choir. Among the
secular works in the library are
pieces unlikely to have been used
by the choristers and one wonders
if the waites might have played
the dances and fantasias for
strings by Simpson and Phillips, or
sung the drinking songs and catches
by Mr Byrd, Mr Purcell, Dr Blow,
and "Jerry Clark" of Trumpet
Voluntary fame.

The York waites were accustomed
to be employed by the 4th Earl of
Cumberland, and his household
accounts recorded that he paid them
thirteen shillings and four pence
to play at the newly-built
Londesborough Hall (about seventeen
miles east of York) in 1612.[61]
Again in 1634 and 1636 they worked
for the Earl and the accounts show
that four horses were sent all the

way to York, from the Earl's main home at Skipton castle, to fetch the John Girdler and the waites for a performance of Francis Beaumont's play "The Knight of the Burning Pestle".[5] The play is a mixed satire, sending up the actors, the establishment of the city of London, and tradesmen, especially grocers. It contains snippets of many popular songs with the words modified to suit the plot, along with instructions for musical interludes.

That the Earl should have sent to York for his musicians is a favourable reflection of the waites' skill and renown. That there were waites of any sort to play the music must have encouraged some jolly banter or even slight changes to the script for in the prologue the "stately music of shawms" is called for and the waites of Southwark recommended as likely suppliers. York had not heard a shawm band for nearly fifty years at the time, but Girdler and company may have had some fun pretending. The Girdler family's instrument collection included a shawm, the "treble howby" listed among Thomas Girdler's posessions on his death in 1645. Perhaps they dug out this elderly instrument for the Skipton show.

Among the tunes in the play were "Goe From My Window", "Fortune My Foe", "With a Fading" (pronounced fah-ding) and several of the catches published by Thomas Ravenscroft in 1609 and 1611, all of which must have been familiar to our waites.

"Goe From My Window"

"With a Fading"

"Fortune My Foe"

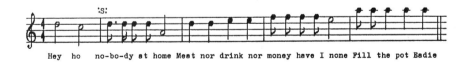

Hey ho   no-bo-dy at home Meat nor drink nor money have I none Fill the pot Eadie

A Ravenscroft Catch

The York city archives contain a singular diary by councillor William Cochrane in which he describes in detail the ceremonies for Mayor making, the King's birthday, and the sheriffs' ridings in the years 1780-6. At these events, he wrote that the waites played "Joys to Great Caesar", a tune which first appeared in England (1683) in a political song in support of Charles the second:

> Joy to Great Caesar,
> Long Life, Love and Pleasure;
> 'Tis a Health that Divine is,
> Fill the Bowl high as mine is:
> Let none fear a Feaver,
> But take it off thus boys;
> Let the King Live for Ever,
> 'Tis no matter for us Boys.

from: Several New Songs by Thomas D'Urfey, 1684. (also in[13])

In 17th century France the tune was known as "Les Folies D'Espagne" (in Spain, "La Folia") but on its arrival in England it became "Farrinel's Ground", named after the violinist Michel Farinelli who used it as the basis of some popular variations. In England both the ground bass and the melody were, rather confusingly, known by this name. A long list of distinguished composers were inspired to make use of this tune, including Lully, Scarlatti, Corelli, Gay, Bach, Grètry, Salieri, Cherubini, Lizst, Nielsen, and Rakhmaninov.[23,36]

Cochrane frequently states that the waites played "Joys to Great Caesar all the time" during a ceremony, something for which this music is ideally suited, the simple ground and melody being infinitely variable for the delight of the players who could revel in continuous extemporisation.

"Les Folies D'Espagne"
a setting for oboes and bassoon by JB Lully of Farrinel's Ground (inset)

About the time he was appointed Minster organist in 1756 John Camidge senior was also given charge of the "city's music", the waites.[28] It is unlikely that he was a regular player in the band, (though he had learned the violin as well as the organ, and a miniature portrait of him exists depicting him in the scarlet coat of a waite) but he certainly arranged and composed the waites' music. The Prince of Wales and the Duke of York visited in 1789 to go to the races, and for the occasion Camidge composed a polonaise for the waites to play. The Prince was so taken by the tune that he contacted the Lord Mayor thanking him profusely and Camidge sent a copy down to London for the future king George IV who presented it to his band of the guards. It is still used by the RAF as a slow march, "The Duke of York's March". Most of the above information is condensed from a letter from Matthew Camidge[52] to the Yorkshire Gazette of 1876 and quoted in "Mr Nobody's Gossip" column in the Yorkshire Evening Press, 1959.[47] It ends:

The old city waits, who now represent the old corporation band, can produce many fine old tunes which they played at Christmastide, composed by this John Camidge, as also can the York Freemasons.

Where are these tunes now? The author is unable to locate them and, at present, the York Freemasons' archivist is assiduously searching his shelves. Only Camidge's sacred works and this piano setting by TP Cooper[9] of the march opposite are readily available.

In 1802 the waites played "God Save the King" on the steps of the Minster and, not surprisingly, the same tune is found at the head of a list among the tunes alongside the loyal toasts for a Mayor making ceremony. This scrap of light blue paper, written written on about 1816, is among many odd documents in the possession of the city archives.[27]

The King
Duke of York
Army and Navy
Earl of Liverpool & Co.
Field Marshall the Duke of Wigan
Major General Sir John Byng
Lords Lieutenants
The Arch Bishop
Members for the County
Members for the City
Prosperity to the City
Major Madox
The Lord Mayor &
The Lady Mayoress

God Save The King
Duke of York's New March
Rule Brittania (sic)
Roast Beef of Old England
See the Conquering Hero Comes
He was Fancied for deeds of Arms
Red Cross Knights
Hush ye pretty warbling Choir
The Nightingale
The Linnet
Hearts of Oak
Patricks Day

here is a health to all good lasses

There can be little doubt that this is a list of instructions to steer the waites through the event. The author can affirm from his own experience that a band of waites always has a list of suitable tunes for reference at a banquet, in fact The York Waits have themselves used such lists in the waites' gallery at The Mansion House in recent times. The sad truth is that such lists are frequently found to have been left at home!

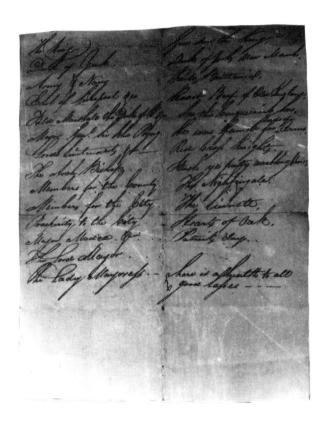

The scrap of blue paper

WAITES' CLOTHING

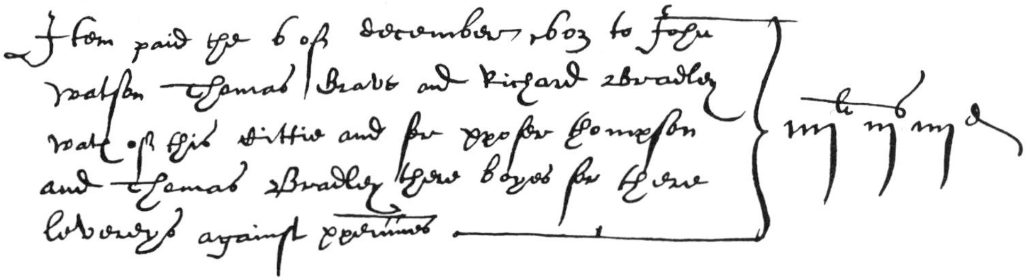

Item paid the 6 of December 1603 to John
Watson Thomas Grave and Richard Bradley
Wates of this Cittie and for Xpofer* thompson
and Thomas Bradley there boyes for there
levereys against Xpenmes*** } iiij^{li} iij^s iiij^d**

*   Christopher
**   £4.3s.4d
*** Christenmes

City Chamberlains' accounts, 1603

   Throughout the York city records from 1442 there is evidence that the
waites were clothed (liveried) by the corporation. The late 15th century
waites wore garments made from striped cloth and light blue (sometimes red)
melde (a cheap cloth of mixed wools).[26,63] Sixteenth century records prove
that the waites received their clothing allowance although we are not told
what they wore until the 1590s. From then until 1836 it is plain that they
wore scarlet livery coats, presumably over their own ordinary clothing.
(see references 15,26,27,28,63) On their coats the waites wore their
scutcheons, badges embroidered with the city arms and the initials of
the Lord Mayor of the time.

Scutcheon

Of their headgear little has been noted. They would almost certainly have worn smart hats, those in fashion at the time, and, perhaps in some periods they were supplied with uniform hats by their employers:

...to Mr John Hillary for trimming ye Silver Hat Lace for the Waites lining etc. for their coates as ye Hats.

Chamberlains' accounts, Nov. 1703[63]

It is thanks to the city surgeon Francis Drake writing in 1736[12] that we are made aware that the uniform of the chief waite included a red hat:

Thefe are preceeded by the city's waites, or muficians, in their fcarlet liveries and filver badges playing all the way through the ftreets.   One of thefe waites wearing on his head a red pinked or tattered ragged cap, a badge of fo great antiquity, the rife or original of it cannot be found out.

Subsequent authors have, perhaps hastily, taken the above to mean that this hat was worn throughout history, but the evidence is fragmentary. We have the advantage over Drake, for there **is** an early reference to it in the city chamberlains accounts two hundred years before he wrote EBORACUM. That was in 1539: the "old red hoode Iagged for one of the eldest wayttes to weyre".[26] After Drake it reappears in the revival of the sheriff's riding in 1819[48] (see appendix III). For the intervening three hundred years there is no concrete basis for the idea that the chief always wore this archaic badge of office.

How to wear an old red hood: 15th, 16th, and 18th century styles

In 1566, when the waites were increased from three to four,[26] a new silver collar or chain was added to the existing three which were worn about the waites' necks. A fifth was ordered to be made in 1770. The city arms hung from these chains, the links of which were the same leopards (lions passant guardant) as on the scutcheon. The three 16th century chains, with some later modifications are still among the Mansion House treasures. They are brought out on civic occasions to be worn, not by today's Waits, but by the mace and sword bearers. Many of the leopards in the chains have been replaced (the chamberlains bought two new "lybartes" in 1592/3[63]) and the number reduced. Could it be that some unscrupulous waites of the past "spent" part of their uniform?

The illustrations throughout this book have been carefully selected so that the clothing of all characters is as near as possible to that worn by the ordinary man in England at the dates given. It is to be hoped that students of costume will find little or nothing to fault.

The author as John Watson, ca 1598 proudly sporting one of the original waites' chains

[NB: The Mansion House Spider Plant and grandfather clock are a touch anachronistic]

THE LIVES OF THE PROFESSIONAL MUSICIANS IN YORK

1304-1896

PART I - YORK'S EARLIEST MINSTRELS AND WAITES

"When the table was y-drawe, Theo Wayte gan a pipe blawe".

Anon. 14th Century

The contest between York's earliest musicians for the title 'first' has
raged long, though hardly savagely, throughout the development of this book.
Just as typesetting began the author received intelligence that one "**Thomas
le Wayte in Walmegate**" (a York street) had been a witness to a property sale
in 1304.

Thomas, then has precedence by fifteen years over the previously-
established number one - Willelmus de Burgh, admitted to the roll of
freemen in 1319 to trade as a harper.[7] To be fair, they were more-or-less
contemporaries and, presuming that Thomas was a musician, nay a waite,
they may have even performed together.

If the very first was a waite, and it was the habit of the time for a man
to be named after his home town or profession, then we know that the second
played the harp and the contributions to our tale by this pair are about
equal. It is particularly satisfactory that the instrument of one of the
city's earliest-named music practitioners should have been recorded. The
size and shape of his harp may be estimated by reference to contemporary
illustration, and from that, and some knowledge of the music of the time,
one may imagine the sounds he produced. Two hundred and fifty years later in
1578 one of the searchers of the York guild of musicians was Ambrose Burghe,
also a harper.[8,26] The reader is invited to determine the degree of
coincidence in the fact. In lists of Yorkshire names Burgh(e) is not common.

The next minstrel to gain freedom to trade in the city of York was William
de Lyncoln in 1343.[7] His name suggests that he was not a local man. His
trade is given as "piper" and he would certainly have been a woodwind player
with various flutes and recorders in his collection of instruments. It is

likely that his main instrument, for outdoor playing especially, was the shawm for in England shawms were often called "pipes" specifically, as well as being included in the generic term for woodwind instruments of all sorts (not to forget bagpipes). The wills of some later York musicians illustrate this point:[24]

John Harper, 1539 "Item. I will and bequeath a noys of pipes called shawmes...."

William Hill, 1558 "Item. I give to Robert Husthwaite....the loude trible pipe with the blaike end...."

Rogerus Wayte, another piper, free in 1363, conveniently brings together the name and the profession, giving us confidence that York employed waites over 100 years before their first civic record in the chamberlains' accounts in 1433. The point is illustrated by an entry in the Doncaster records of 1457: "Allan Pyper and William Pyper are elected Pipers or Wayts".[3]

It is claimed here that Thomas le Wayte was the first waite of York for whom we have reasonable evidence....so far.

Thomas le Wayte
or
Roger Wayte

PART II - THE FIFTEENTH CENTURY

"A Wayte....that nightely from Michelmas to Shreve Thorsdaye pipeth the watch within this Courte fowre tymes, in somers nightes iij tymes and makeyth bon gayte at euery chamber doore and offyce as well for fear of pyckers and pillars".

Anon. pre-1483

**John de Styllington
An early 15th century musician**

In his Oxford Companion to Music,[39] Percy Scholes gives the first mention of the York waites as 1272. Lyndesay Langwill quotes 1369.[29] In the author's experience there are only hints to their existence before 1434, such as Thomas le- and Roger Wayte and records of regular payments to "the minstrells" from 1370 or 1371 onwards. The city chamberlains' roll of 1433 gives the number of city minstrels as three: "trium ministrallorum ciuitatis" and in the following year for the first time calls them the waites: "lez waytes civitatis", characteristically using the bureaucratic, "macaronic" language, a mixture of Norman French, English, and Latin.[63]

libata yemals de		liberata yemalis de (winter liveries)
lez Waytes civitats	or	lez Waytes civitatis
Sm⸝ XXvij^s X^d		Summa XXvij^s X^d (27s:10d)

"In Dei Nomine Amen Penultimate day of February 1483 John Shene, citizen and wate of york of the parish of St Helen's on the walls....".

So begins the will[22] of York's first named waite, a minstrel free in 1440.[7] Had he bequeathed instruments we would have had an idea of his activity. However he did mention the two mills that he built on the moor between York and Heworth, indicating that he was quite a wealthy man. Here he is playing the **hurdy-gurdy**, a popular instrument only known in York from the medieval churches of St Denys and St Olave.

The fifteenth century saw the passing of a number of musicians (appendix I) whose careers are totally obscure, though there are occasional tantalising glimpses of their lives, such as: John Swynbourne, whose will is the earliest, but gives away nothing, and overleaf........

**John Swynbourne:
The art of courtly love
in York during the reign
of Richard III, 1485**

....**Ricardus Twysday "mynstrall et brewer"** free 1493.[7]

The minute books of the common council chamber first name a waite in 1486.[26] The musician was Robert Comgilton, (who was probably the Robert Comylton free 1486,[7] and also Robert Comolton whose will of 26th Sept 1508 is indexed but did not reach probate and is now lost).[24]

.... Robert Comgilton one of the waites of this citie to be admitted to the roume of Robert Sheyne, being in so grete age and so decrepid that he ne may forther attend thoccupation of waite aforesaid.[26]

So Robert Sheyne was too elderly to pursue his profession, and Comgilton was drafted in as his replacement. Was Sheyne the Shene without a christian name in the freemens' roll of 1484, and was this Shene related (brother perhaps) to John Shene, mentioned above?

In 1486, Robert Lemyngton and William Plombre received their freedom concurrently with Robert Comylton.[7] During the previous ten years only "Shene" had been recorded in the roll of freemen. It seems likely that the city had need of new waites and that these three were appointed together.

PART III - THE SIXTEENTH CENTURY-

ONE HUNDRED YEARS OF THE SHAWM BAND

CITIZEN: What stately music have you? You have shawms?
PROLOGUE: Shawms? No.
CITIZEN: No? I'm a thief if my mind did not give me so. Rafe plays a stately part, and he must needs have shawms; I'll be at the charge of them myself, rather than we'll be without them.
PROLOGUE: So you are like to be.
CITIZEN: Why, and so I will be. There's two shillings; let's have the waites of Southwark. They are as rare fellows as any are in England; and that will fetch them o'er the water with a vengeance, as they were mad.

Francis Beaumont, 1607

John Harper, fl. 1514-39
One of York's Tudor waites

Roger Smalwode, free 1503,[7] was employed as a civic minstrel in 1505.[26] When, for how long, and with whom John Harper, free 1514,[7] was a waite is unclear, but he would have served during the 1530s and his will of 1539 provides fine evidence of a three-man shawm band in York:[24]

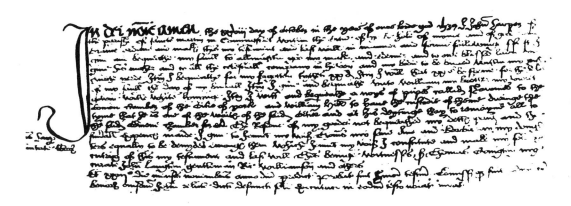

Item. I will and bequeath a noys of pipes called shawmes to the comon chamber of the Citie of York and William Hill to have the custodie of them duringe the tyme that he is one of the waites of the said Citie and at his departinge they to remayne all to the said comon chambre for ever.

William Hill became chief waite in about 1545, and Harper's shawms may have been those featured in his will of 1558 (see below).[24] They then reappear in the city records of 1565:[26]

Memorandum the xxth day of May anno 1565 Thomas Mower one of the Waites of the citie haith delyveryd to the chambre of Owsebrige by the commaundment of my Lorde Mayour one pype or instrument callyd a shawme with a case of ledder for the same that was geven to this citie by Iohn Harper sometyme one of the waites of this citie.

The last appearance of John Harper's shawms is in the council house books in a memorandum of 4th dec 1566:[26]

It was agred by the said presens that where there be a noyse of iiij^{or}*
shalmes** in Mr Dyneley*** handes whiche hath at solempne tymes ben
used by the waytes within this citie and nowe are lyke to be sold forth
of the same citie Except meanes to be made for steying of the same
within this citie it is therfor aggreed that there shall be gyven for
the said noyse of the chambre money xls.**** And to be saffly kept to
the citie commonalitie.

*   4
**   the fourth was a 'base shalme' bought for eleven shillings in 1576
***   John Dynelay, draper and lord mayor in 1576
**** Forty shillings

So Harper's shawms were used by the waites from before 1539 until after 1566, when some time towards the end of the century the more fashionable cornetts and saggbuts took over (ca 1585-90). In York shawms seem to have been completely abandoned whereas in other regions, especially on the continent, they remained popular outdoor instruments, often played in consort with cornetts and saggbuts.

Finally it may be considered that this same "noyse of shalmes" may have been heard by Henry VIII on his visit in 1541, when the three waites led by William Hill played at the welcoming pageant at Micklegate Bar. (A pretty picture, but I fear it may not be presumed that they were there).

A Noyse of Shawms in the hands of The York Waits

It was at this time that we first discover the York waites on tour. The household accounts of Henry Manners, Earl of Rutland, recorded their visits in the Decembers of 1539 and 1540 when the three waites perhaps played for pre-Christmas celebrations at Belvoir Castle. It was quite the general rule that waites would visit other cities or private households. Those of York did so as above, at Nottingham in the late sixteenth century, and at Londesborough and Skipton for the Earls of Cumberland in the early seventeenth. Most city records give long lists of payments to waites from all over England but the York records have none. Throughout historical times York's freedom laws and the ordinances of the musicians guild were notorious for excluding all but Royal musicians. No outside waites ever played legally in York.

In the 1540s it is possible for the first time to deduce the names of all of the waites: William Hill, Henry Knyght, and Nicholas Wright.[7,26] John Harper seems to have been active at least until the writing of his will in October 1539.[24] He died twenty five days later on 22nd Nov and, although William Hill's name does not appear in the city records (except for his freedom in 1536) until 1544, that Harper should elect him custodian of his precious shawms implies that Hill was to succeed him as chief waite. Just after Harper's death one Henry Knyght received his freedom to practice specifically as "wayte" (1541). His term of office may have been short, for he appears in no other records. Nicholas Wright, free 1546, was probably the third waite around 1550 though he does not appear in the city records until a few months after Hill's death; then it would seem that he was already the senior waite:[26]

Item payd to Nycholas Wright and his two ffellos waites of this citie....

It is inferred from Hill's will (1558) that shortly before his death he was chief waite, assisted by Wright and Robert Husthwaite (free 1558).[7] The long and complicated will bequeathes a coat and an instrument apiece to three men who must surely have been the next waites band:[24]

Item I give to Robert Husthwaite my reade [red] jacket and the loude trible pipe with the blaicke end [soprano shawm?] that the said Robert hathe plaide the morn wathches withe.

Item I give to my fellowe Nicholas [Wright?] my marble jacket and a sharpe quatrible pipe for the still noyse.

Item I give to Thomas [Mower/Moore?] my brother son my best baggepipe and xxs in money.

The second entry above begs the question: what was the "pipe for
the still noyse"? The only applicable meaning for 'still' is quiet, as in
'a still small voice'. There is mention of "still shalms" in the inventory
of Henry VII's instruments 1509,[61] but exactly what they may have been
is uncertain. The wreck of Henry VIII's flagship, the Mary Rose, may have
provided the answer, for among the artefacts recovered was a singular
shawm with a cylindrical, rather than the usual conical bore. It would have
certainly have been much quieter than a usual shawm. Was it the mysterious
"doucaine" or perhaps a "still shawm"?

**Moore, Husthwaite & Wright with the instruments bequeathed them
by William Hill**

St. Helen, Stonegate.

William Hill was quite a well-to-do figure in the parish of St Helen in Stonegate. He bequeathed to his daughter Jennet, wife of Christofer Willoughbye, his house with cellars, shops, stables, yard, and gardens. He also had let an annexe of his house known as "Paradise Chambre" to Willoughbye and wished it to become the property of his second daughter Margaret Dawson. He had property let to Margaret Husthwaite (related to Robert, the waite?) and his own house must have been quite lavishly decorated for he left to Peter Dawson "all the paynted clothes and hanginges therefrom".[24]

The council house books, in a minute of 23rd may 1561, names all three waites: Nicholas Wright, Robert Husthwaite, and Thomas Mower. The last was not pulling his weight:[26]

It is ordered that the same Thomas shall have respit to learne and applie himself in the instrumentes and songes belongyng to the sayd waytes and to leave his unthrifty gamying upon peyne to be putt forth of that office for ever.

Nicholas Wright pulls
Thomas Moore's leg as
that unfortunate waite
prepares to face the
ire of My Lord Mayor.

So in 1561 there was a three-man band of waites playing shawms and bagpipe on the morn watches, or to awaken citizens on request, and providing grand music for pompous civic processions and banquets.

After Wright, Husthwaite became head waite and the new recruit was Arthure Hodgeson whose career lasted for at least sixteen years, though he never attained the senior post, as did Moore some time after 1571. Moore's career lasted about twenty one years.

A council house book minute of 30th Oct 1566 states: "....the common waytes of this citie are dicharged of their office", but the reason is not given.[26] Perhaps it was Husthwaite who was held responsible for the misdemeanour, for he was the only one not re-employed in April 1567 when the newly-appointed Robert Hewet (Hewit or Hewyt) was ordered to reform the band, from thenceforth with four players. Hewet, Hodgeson, and Moore were joined by a musician not named at the time. The freemens' roll of 1566 names John Balderston as "waite" so in all probability it was he. Three years later there was unrest amongst the waites and Hogeson, Moore, and Balderston were warned to be "of good abearing to one an oyer".[26] On 27th May 1575 it was reported that "Arthure Hodgeson late one of the waites of this Citie and discharged shalbe one of the foure waites of this Citie agayne...to be placed the second man". Evidently there was more strife in the band, a characteristic of this particular group of musicians: sacked, 1566; warned, 1569; one sacked ca 1574; all sacked again, 1572; and Balderston and Clerke sacked in 1584. Every dismissal seems somehow to have involved John Balderston, though he was rarely held responsible. One is tempted to conclude that he was not an evil man, but one easily led by his less responsible elders, and perhaps he had a hasty temper. One may only day-dream the personalities of these gentlemen, represented as they are by mere scraps of cold, historical record (as I'm afraid I do!).

Hewet led a mysterious career, in and out of the waites over the twenty four year period 1567-1592.[26,59] He seems to have been drafted in at intervals to reorganise the city band when things became chaotic or when there was the need of another player, but was rarely a full-time waite for long. In 1603, though he was no longer a waite, he was still around acting as guarantor for young York musicians seeking their freedom to practice their trade in the city. In 1587 he (or perhaps another Hewet) was rewarded by the Minster chaplains for supplying or copying "certaine songes for the queare" and in 1592 he was paid two shillings by the Shuttleworth family at Smithills, Lancs. It has been suggested[58] that he went alone on this occasion, wearing his city livery, and thus became recorded as waite of York rather than simply as a minstrel. There is but one blot on his otherwise impeccable record: in 1565 he was presented before the searchers of the guild of minstrells for playing at a freemens' dinner, which was forbidden in that guild's ordinances.

It would have been Robert Hewet who led the waites on their visits to Nottingham in 1569, 1578, 1579 and 1582. In 1579 they called twice in, June and September, and Woodfill[61] has concluded that they perhaps spent the intervening period in the south, stopping off at Nottingham on their way home. Nottingham, of course, had its own waites who, we may hope, did not resent the presence of rivals from the one city in the realm that would not entertain outsiders.

In 1578 the ancient ordinances of the guild of musicians, a relatively new body set up between 1554 and 1561;[58] came under the scrutiny of the aldermen and privy council of York.[26] At that time the master of the guild was Robert Hewit (one time ordinance-breaker) and the searchers the aforesaid harper, Ambrose Burghe and Cuthbert Watson, a musician free 1554, and father of the noted waite John Watson (fl. 1591-1622).

The ordinances (see appendix V) laid out in great detail the rules for York's musicians, protecting members from competition from outside the city and from each other. No musician could play after 9pm and only the waites had the right to play "huntsups". The waites were obliged to take the early morning watch, assuring the citizens of their safety in the night and playing to mark the hours. They could be hired by house-holders to play noisy aubades to awaken the occupants and these alarm-call tunes became known as "huntsups", by association with the early rising of hunt participants and with a popular tune of that name, variously: "ye Hunte yis Uppe", "Huntsup" or in a Newcastle manuscript "Honsup". The popularity of this tune lasted from the 1530s until well into the 17th century and fragments of it have been identified in Cumbrian folk song in this century.[56]

*****

"**Jac**: *Hark, are the waites abroad?*
 Fab: *Be softer prithee, 'tis private musick.*
 Jac: *Well I will hear, or sleep, I care not whether!*"

                                                                        John Fletcher, 1625

*****

In the pageant of Corpus Christi (now known as the York cycle of mystery plays) the musicians took the play of "Harowld (Herod) his sone two counsellors and the messinger enquirynge the iij (3) kinges of the childe Iesu" (until 1561 performed by the masons). The only music to survive from the 16th century mystery plays are three dreary vocal pieces in the weavers' play. It is a pity that no music of the York musicians' play should have lasted.[41]

The last pageant of Corpus Christi was staged in 1567. By then the protestant church had established itself in York and such old papist traditions suppressed. York's citizens still had the need to participate in some great ceremony of their own and the corporation developed the "Midsomereven Show", a public display of the arms and armour maintained by each parish in case of strife. The accounts of the earliest (1584-5) of these great shows were particularly detailed and a picture of the whole procession is possible:

Firstly, two days before the event, the waite John Balderston took his fife and, accompanied by the city drummer Edmund Archer, (not "Arther" as given in REED[26])[58] went about the city "to warn the citizens" of the coming event. At dawn on Midsummer eve every able-bodied man his donned armour, shouldered pike, halberd, or matchlock, and marched behind his parish constable to St George's Field (in later years the Knavesmire). There, the three or so of them were marshalled into one long procession headed by the two sheriffs and the great silk standard, "the auncient" of York. Around the standard two handsword players twirled and flourished their ceremonial weapons, so enthusiastically that one of them accidentally slashed the flag, a mistake which cost the chamberlains a shilling for repairs.

For music two drummers were present, one was Edmund Archer with **the** drum, the great drum

The
Standard
Bearer

painted with the city's arms, and the other, anonymous, with "the litle drum". Both instruments had new heads and snares for the 1584 procession. The drummers were accompanied by the city trumpeter and somewhere in the front part of the procession came the four city waites in their new liveries delivered that year to Robert Hewit, head waite at the time. The others were John Balderston, John Clerke and George Cowper. The last was a southerner from Ipswich, employed in May 1584 and sacked in October for his part in a case of fraud. The waites almost certainly would have played shawms for the event, perhaps still using John Harper's "noyse".

The procession and inspection being over the Lord Mayor and his staff returned to the guildhall to watch a wagon play by school master John Grafton, during which they all enjoyed (at the city's expense) several hundred apples, ten pounds of sugar, five pounds of "marmalaid" plenty of "fyne suckett, carrawais & biskyttes, maynebread & cakes", washed down with fourteen gallons of ale, seven and a half gallons of wine and claret, and a gallon of sack![26,27]

The next anecdote has no bearing on York music whatsoever but is well worth relating. An able-bodied man who did not attend the midsummer muster would be obliged to face the Lord Mayor and any penalty resulting therefrom. Such a man was Robert Paycock, merchant who appeared at the common chamber, on 16th July:[26]

And now Robert Pacock merchant being one of the persons which hath made default at the midsummer show, personally appeared at the counsell chambre upon Ousebridge before these present and was fined six sillings and eight pence, which he paid, and had three shillings and fourpence given him [back] again.
    And now the said Robert spake and said openly before, and to these pre-

The Midsomer Even Show, 1584

sent these unfitting and unseemly words: 'I have bought a halberd which cost me 20 shillings and it is so much dearer than this three shillings and fourpence which I have now paid. And I will sell it and never come at that show while I live; fine me twenty shillings if ye will!'

Whereupon it is now agreed that the said Robert Paycock shall pay twenty shillings for a fine forthwith or else be committed to gaol for a space of two months.

On 21st Oct 1584 two more waites were sacked:[24]

....John Clarke and Baltherston two of the waites of this cittie did personallie appere in this court, and were examined towching their evill and disorderlie behaviour, to the discredit of this cittie viz. for that they haue gone abroad, in the contry in very evill apparell, with their hose forth at their heeles, also for that they are comon drunkerdes and cannot so conynglie play on their instrumentes as they ought to do, and concerning other their misdemeanour, which disorder the said wates cold not deny wherupon and for the worshipp of the said cittie, it is agreed by these presentes that the said Clarke and Baltherston shalbe presentlie dischardged of their office of wates, and their badges to be taken from them, and other sufficient men to be chosen in their places such as shalbe in this court...

Their sentences must have been suspended, for both of the miscreants continued in the service of the city as waites for some time after.

Under Hewet, and until the end of the 16th century, the waites' personnel

changed frequently. The Balderston family was prominent in York life, John being a long-serving waite and his son Peter, a tiler, the city's pageant master. Arthure Hodgeson's apprentice, John Clerke became a full member of the band around 1572 and remained there until he was too old to continue in 1596.[26]

....with their hose forth at their heeles

Until the research for this book began the author could remember just two dates of great events in British History. The first 1066, may not concern us but the other 1588, had a little effect on York and a great deal on waites (though not those of York, read on). King Phillip of Spain decided to put an end to war with Queen Elizabeth by sending a great fleet of ships (the Spanish Armada) to conquer England. Preparations to repel the Spaniards were made nationally and the port of Hull requested the cities in its region to supply ships or money. The city of York refused and, what's more got away with playing virtually no part in the famous defeat of the Armada. Then in 1596 the Cadiz expedition was organised, and this time York was obliged to contribute a ship, the Elizabeth Jonas by name. York also provided some crew members including the cook, the surgeon, and the trumpeter. It is, of course, the last who is of great interest to us for he was York's city trumpeter, by profession almost a city waite, for he was liveried similarly and wore a silver cognisance and would have appeared at the same official functions as the waites.

The trumpeter's name was Edward Millington and his first recorded appearance is as trumpeter to a merchant named Robert Asshe. He was taking his freedom in 1595 as an inholder, that is an ale-house or inn keeper, the second trade of many a poor York musician at the time. In the following year he was city trumpeter on his way to Cadiz (or "Cales" as the records have it) in the fleet of ninety-six English ships under the command of The Lord Admiral, (Charles Howard) Lord Thomas Howard, The Earl of Essex, and Sir Walter Raleigh. Fireships were sent into the Spanish fleet, caught unawares moored in Cadiz harbour, destroying the enemy's navy before they could put to sea. One can imagine Millington lustily (or sea-sick and terrified) blasting signals on his trumpet above the roar of cannon and the cries of fighting men.

On his return to York Millington was paid at the rate of five pounds per month (twenty five pounds) and given twenty shillings compensation by the

city council. In the years after Cadiz he seems to have been constantly in debt whereas he might have been comfortably-off, for a while at least, if he had had the opportunity to join in the pillaging of the defeated city. It seems that Raleigh was a man to encourage just that, but had a row with Essex on the subject whilst at Cadiz. Essex's men were forbidden to go ashore and one wonders if Millington could have been one of them. It is, of course possible to return from one's pillaging empty-handed for having over-indulged in alternative aspects of that activity!

It is evident that Millington went abroad again for:[26]

Also it is agreed that Edward Millington Trumpiter shall have given hym forth of the common chambre against Christenmas next xiiijs iijd [13s:4d] towardes his releif in regard he hath bene of late prisoner and captive vnder the Turkes.

Just who these "Turkes" were is not given. At that date even Spaniards could be called Turks.

There is little more about Edward Millington but payments of wages, and accounts of livery and relief from his lifetime's poverty until the end.[11,63] He died in June 1644 after almost fifty years as the York city trumpeter, and was buried at the church of Holy Trinity in Goodramgate. After his death the council sought to recover his official badge which would have been of silver, bearing the arms of York. His daughter had to be given the ten shillings necessary to redeem it from the pawn-broker.

As promised above something must be said of the effect upon waites of the war with Spain. The waites in question were not from York for that city, to a man, ducked responsibility of defence against the Armada. These were the famous Norwich waites who went with Sir Francis Drake on his expedition to Lisbon in 1589. In a letter to the mayor of Norwich he reqested that the waites accompany him and the decision of the city council to permit this was minuted thus:[42]

This daye was redd in the court A letter to Mr Maior and his brethren from Sir Frauncys Drake whereby he desyreth that the waytes of this citie may bee sent to hym to go the new intendid voyage whervnto the waytes beeyng here called doo all assent whervpon it is agreed that they shall have vj [6] cloakes of stamell cloath made them redy before they go And that a wagon shalbe provided to carry them and there instrumentes And that they shall haue iiijli [£4] to buye them Three new howboyes [shaums] & one treble Recorder and xli [£10] to beare their chardgys And that the citie shall hyer the wagon & paye for it Also that the chamberleyn shall paye Peter Spratt xs [10 shillings] for a Saquebutte Case And the waytes to delyuer to the Chamberleyn before they go the Cities cheanes.

The waites who went with Drake were Robert Thacker, Peter Spratt, Jamys Wyllson, Thomas Mannyng, and Arthur Jackson (odd that these five should have required six new coats). Sadly, especially for the waites, the expedition was not a great success and three of them perished, only Spratt and Jackson returning to Norwich.

It is interesting to speculate that had York been involved, and had Drake heard of the York waites (who were surely the equals of the Norwich band) that John Clerke, Thomas Grave, William Johnson, and Christopher Dent could have had the opportunity to sail away and die for Queen and country, and to be immortalised in Alfred Noyes' epic poem "Drake" but that privilege belonged to their counterparts in Norwich:[42]

For oft had Spaniards brought a rumour back
Of that strange pirate who in royal state
Sailed to the sound of violins, and dined
With skilled musicians round him, turning all
Battle and storm and death into a song.

Thomas Grave(s), mentioned above began his term as waite around 1587-8 and soon became chief of a band which included William Johnson (whose stay was rather short) and Christofer Dent, who died in 1592 allowing John Watson to embark upon his distinguished career. Cuthbert Thompson and Christofer Smyth were both in the band in 1593 but gone by 1602, Thompson having "...gone abrode into the contry without licenc of My Lord Maiour ..."[26] He had presumably resigned for he handed over to the council his chain and cognisance before leaving, but he soon returned to York in 1603, joining forces with John Clerke (by then ex-waite, see below) and Robert Sympson (an ordinary musician). They must have tried to form a band of alternative waites for they were "presented" to the council for punishment for playing a Huntsup contrary to the ordinances. This task was specifically for the official waites.[58]

A memorandum in the council's house book for 17th Dec 1600 offers an amusing picture of the waites over-employment:[26]

and wheras the wates haue put in a peticion in regard that two or three of the aldermen do make ther befe breakfast in some one mornyng all at one tyme so as they cannot convenientlie serue them all that either they wold make ther breakfastes seuerall dayes or ells that the said waites may be discharged of that service....

Their desires were met with a practical compromise. The waites of the time were almost certainly those named in the chamberlains' accounts of 1602 noting their clothing allowance: Thomas Graves, John Watson, Cuthbert Thompson, Richard Bradley, and Christofer Thompson (apparently not related to Cuthbert), "and ther boye".

John Watson, free 1591,[8] was appointed to the York waites in 1592 to replace the deceased Christofer Dent of whom virtually nothing can be discovered. Watson joined the band in the last years of the ageing, deaf, drunkard John Clerke, one of the longest-serving of all the waites of the time (25 years). The unfortunate Clerke was "retired" in 1596 by the council at the request of his colleagues who complained that:[26]

....he is become so disordred and distemppred and such a person as wilbe verie oft dronk and is at diuerse tymes trobled with the falling sicknesse and his hearing unperfit or almost deaf as that he is not sufficient to serve his place.

Kindly, the waites put up an annual pension of 26s:8d.

PART IV – _THE SEVENTEENTH CENTURY –_

CORNETTS AND SAGGBUTS

"At supper in Lichfield the musicians [for fidlers I must not call them] were the Gentlemen Waytes of the Towne, that wore the badge of a Noble brave Lord, and they were of that garb, and skill, as they were fitting to play to the nicest eares".

Anon. 1634

"His Lordship and the guests being all seated, the City-Music begin to touch their Instruments with very Artfull fingers".

Thos. Jordan, 1680

A Jacobean waite with pipe & tabor

Until John Clerke's dismissal the new fashion was that there should be
five waites, but under the direction of the experienced Graves, John Watson,
Richard Bradley, and young Christofer Thompson (Watson's apprentice)
continued as a quartet until the appointment of John Bradley (incorrectly
named Thomas in some sources), nephew of Richard, who inherited his
uncle's instruments in 1623: "...my treble cornett my saggbut and my base
viall...."[24]

It was the quintet named above who played for the visit of James I & VI
on 16th April, 1603:[26]

Also it is agreed that the waites shall play at Micklithbarr at the
receivinge of the kinges maiestie to this Cittye, and after they shall
have done ther then to go over the Water at lendinge & thorowe the
mintgarth to Bartholomew Applebyes howse and so to Bowthome Barr, and
that ther shalbe a scafield maide within Barr for them to stand and playe
on.

Their journey across York from Micklegate Bar to Bootham Bar may have been

quite a scramble for they were to play in a dignified manner for their king at both stations, having taken a longer and more difficult route than his majesty. They played well that day as is reported in the account of the King's visit in the back of council house book number 32:

...trumpittes beinge standinge upon the battlement of Micklith barr without the same barr sounded mostt cheirfullye until his Maiestie came neare this cittye, and then this cittyes waites sounded up ther lowde instrumentes in the best sorte they coulde...

Very few, if any, of the citizens would ever have seen a monarch (the last royal visit had been made by Henry VIII in 1541) and King James was sensitive to this when he was to go the short distance from his overnight home in the King's Manor to the Minster on the Sunday:[26]

I will Haue no coach, for the people are desirous to see a king, and so they shall, for they shall aswell see his body as his face.

There is sufficient information available for a very clear picture of the waites on this very splendid occasion to be postulated. They wore the clothing of the ordinary Jacobean man over which they donned their scarlet livery coats. Their city badges, embroidered in silver and gold thread would have carried the initials "R W" of Lord Mayor Sir Robert Watter (donor to the city of the Lady Mayoress's chain and whose splendid painted tomb, bearing the effigies of him and his family is now installed in the little hall built on the site of St Crux Church). Around their necks they hung their waites chains. It is also possible to to make an intelligent guess which instruments were played and by whom.

In 1602 the council lent John Watson £4 for the purchase of his "doble curtall".[26]

Besides noting the two occasions on which Watson repaid forty shillings, bang on time, the chamberlains' accounts noted that he took receipt of "a duble curtall or howboy".[63] Here the etymology of early English instruments becomes confused for the latter name was generally used for the shawm of which the curtal was a rather distant relative. Perhaps the chamberlains' clerk knew less of the tools of the music trade than he thought when he scratched the alternative name (clever clogs!). In April 1603 Sir Major (Mauger) Vavasor esq. sold the city one saggbut for £8 for the waites "to be used for the King's visit".[24] The senior waites, Graves and Richard Bradley probably owned their instruments and would not have needed the new saggbut. Anyway it is very likely that they took the more taxing work of playing cornett, a most difficult instrument to play well. That leaves the two young apprentices playing tenor lines on saggbut.

Soprano..Graves.....cornett
Alto.....Bradley R..cornett
Tenor....Thompson...saggbut
Tenor....Bradley T..saggbut
Bass.....Watson......curtal

By 1605 Graves has left the records. His will cannot be found unless it is that of Thomas Graves, singingman (one of the vicars choral, living at the Bedern Hall) dated 18th September 1604.[24] Had Graves the waite also been an officer of the Minster it is possible that the latter trade should have eclipsed the former's importance in his will. The last report of Graves alive was in July 1603, when he was ordered not to dissociate himself from the other waites.[58] Had there been a serious row between him and his colleagues or was the aging Graves become awkward in his last years? In 1605 Christofer Thompson, until then Watson's apprentice, was promoted to his place as a full waite to replace Thomas Graves, deceased. At this time John Watson certainly became the chief waite. Who moved into the lower ranks is impossible to decide. A number of musicians gained their freedom in 1604[8] and any could have been a new waite: Willam Clerke (the son of a waite); Christopher Thomlinson (perhaps Watson's brother-in-law, for his sister was Elizabeth Thomplinson); John Barton (apprentice of Richard Laverock); or George Atkynson (apprentice of Cuthbert Watson).

John Watson died in 1622 and was buried at the delightful Church of Holy Trinity Goodramgate. His will, though of genealogical interest, does not mention his instruments.[24] (see p 104: The Watson/Girdler family pedigree).

Richard Bradley was buried in 1623 in St Michael le Belfrey Church. His will requests that he should be buried: "...as neare my daughter Elizabeth Petty as convenientlie it may be".[24] In 1637 Frances Bradley joined her husband and daughter in the south aisle, but their tombs cannot be found today.

In 1611 the waites seriously offended members of the other guilds with whom they shared St Anthony's Hall by performing "...certaine scandallous libells songes or sonnettes...".[26] Bradley's uncle John lived in Louth, Lincolnshire, and Richard and his wife Frances would visit what may have once been the ancestral home, where he had picked up the offending songs from the Louth waites. He was duly held responsible and hauled up before the council for a roasting. From the entry in the minute book it would seem that the waites did not fancy repenting, but in the end Bradley's, perhaps rather

Richard Bradley, with a borrowed theorbo, hurriedly composing a cleaned-up version of the "certaine libells songes and sonnettes" for My Lord Mayor. NB the original was scribbled on the table cloth.

tongue-in-cheek apology, was sufficient reparation.

The York apprentice register recorded that Richard Bradley himself took on yet another John Bradley as an apprentice musician. Remarkably he was the son of still another John Bradley, this one "de Lin in com. Nor" (of Lynn in the county of Norfolk). In 1612, the year that the York waites (seven of them are mentioned!) were first employed by Francis Clifford, 4th Earl of Cumberland, so were the waites of Kings Lynn.[61] It may just have been that the Bradley family was able to get together, either as a family, or even as musicians. John Bradley senior was pensioned off in 1646 with forty shillings per annum: "...late one of the town (Kings Lynn) waits....aged and decrepid..." (Mss by Henry Mann, vol.II fol.33 in Norwich Public Library).

Our waites went on one of their rather infrequent travels, to play for the Earl of Cumberland (Francis Clifford of Skipton Castle) at his second home of Londesborough Hall a few miles east of York:

28 August 1612: Item given the same day in reward....to the waits of york being seven in number who came to Londsborough and steyed all night and played in the great chamber after supper, 13s:4d.

Seven waites are nowhere else recorded and it **is proposed that** the band of six, including John Watson and Richard Bradley, **took along an** apprentice noted as the seventh by the Earl's accountant.

John Girdler first appears in the city records in 1623 as replacement for the deceased John Watson, and the next recipient of the city's saggbut.[26] He was Watson's son-in-law, having married Janne (Jane) Watson in 1620 at the Church of St Michael le Belfrey. The Watsons lived in the parish of Holy Trinity Goodramgate and the Girdlers settled in St Crux parish, probably after the wedding. The Girdler family seems to have been new to York but they were to become dominant in the city's music for the next half century. Thomas Girdler, certainly John's younger brother and apprentice was, for a short time, one of the waites:

And now it is ordred that Thomas Girdler that hath bene brought upp as an apprentice with John Girdler his brother one of this Citties waites being first admitted to the ffreedome of this Cittye be admitted also to the place of the third waite within this Cittye during the pleasure of this court and upon his good carriage and behaviour. (House Book 35, 1630).

Thomas married Isabel Stradlinge at St Crux in 1634 and an average family was completed by the births of young Thomas and Joanne. It had been thought that that was all that could be discovered of the life and work of the mysterious Girdler brother whose contribution to the city council records was minimal. Then, just before publication, an inventory of his goods, post-mortem, was discovered in the probate index of the Minster Dean and Chapter. The author was informed and what he beheld was the tatty vellum illustrated photographically opposite. Not only was this a detailed list of Thomas Girdler's property at the time of his demise in November 1640: it mentions his clothing of which "3 bands" (falling band collars) and "a paire of ruffes," along with "two reede cloakes" are certainly his formal livery....and then it itemises his instruments, the longest and most list detailed discovered!

his instruments

1	[]	*tribble cornets*
2	[]	*single sackbutt*
3	[]	*treble howby (treble shawm)*
4	[]	*lisserdine (lizard or tenor cornett)*
5	[]	*...orders (recorders)*
6,7		*one treble violin and one tenor*
8,9		*one bandera (bandora) and one kitt*

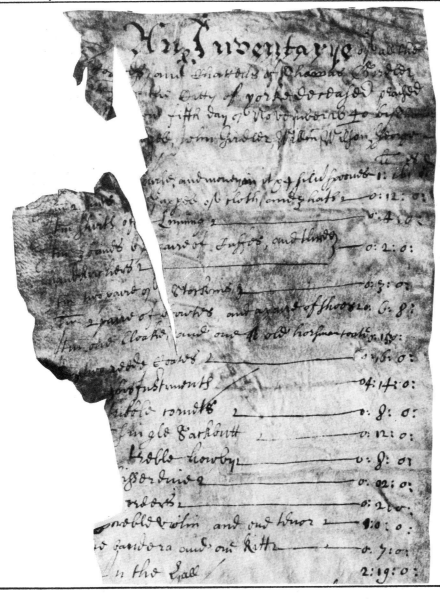

Thomas Girdler's inventory contains the the first York reference to the shawm (treble howby) for over fifty years and there is no way of knowing whether it was an up-to-date, seventeenth century model, foreshadowing the invention of the oboe - due from France in about twenty years - or if it was an elderly instrument, perhaps an antique or heirloom, even one of John Harper's shawms. The lizard has turned up in York for the first, and only time. Its tone was said by Praetorius, writing in 1619 to be "unlovely and horn-like", an apt descrition of an instrument best suited, like its larger cousin the serpent, to accompanying choirs. The Bandora was an English invention from 1561, steel strung and used as an accompaniment to solo singers. The kitt was a delightful small fiddle or rebec, very portable and frequently the source of music for a dancing master.

From the above inventory and dicussion a good deal of inferences may be made about the musical activities of Thomas Girdler: bandsman, chamber musician, Minster musician, accompanist, and perhaps dancing master.

Opposite: **Thomas Girdler's Instruments.**
The numbers refer to the list on page 94

The Girdler family at home, 1645

John Girdler's four sons by Jane all grew up to be professional musicians, Adam and Christopher, (probably Ambrose and Richard too) appointed waites. It is evident that the civil war seriously affected civic life and the waites, not because of puritanism, but simply because of the disruption of life caused by the war.[38] John Girdler continued to lead the band but it seems that he only had his young sons for assistants and only he was paid and liveried. In 1652 the waites were dismissed altogether:[15]

In regard of the extreame poverty of this citty it is ordered that John Gridler [sic] and his sons be hencefourth discharged of walkinge the night watch or performinge any other service or expecting any benefit as the citty waites till further notice.

After what must have been a time of great poverty for the redundant Girdlers the waites (one assumes J Girdler and sons) were reinstated in 1657,[15] but since the chamberlains' accounts mention no wages for them it would seem that the council was either still too poor to pay them, or that they were anxious to be rid of the aging John Girdler and his dynasty (he would, by then have served for 35 years). A house book minute confirms the end of the Girdlers by noting that when the waites make up their number to six their salaries and liveries will be taken into consideration, provided that John Girdler and the rest deliver their chains and badges to their successors (28th Nov 1660). The council had certainly succeeded in replacing the old guard by 1665 (not long before Girdler's death) for 9 yards of scarlet cloth (enough for six livery coats) was purchased for the waites, and Girdler was gone from the council's records. After that there is only his will of 13th Nov 1666, hastily written on his sick-bed, and the record of his burial in the parish church of St Crux:

John Girdler Chefe master of the Cittys waites was buried Nov 66

That may have been the end of the Watson-Girdler family as waites, but they still had a role to play as York musicians after John's death, and some aspects of his sons' lives were recorded:

Of Adam, the eldest, little can be deduced, but that shortly before he was admitted to the freedom of the city (musitian 1638)[8] he was called for, independent of the waites, as an actor to perform in "The Knight of the Burning Pestle" at Skipton castle (see page 36). Which role would have suited this young man, aged about eighteen years? It is impossible to say. The main company of actors is reputed to have been the Queens players, so perhaps, with professionals present, one of the smaller parts was available for our York man. Maybe he got the job simply by his dad's influence. John himself was there with three other waites to provide the music for the play. Christopher is the only son mentioned by name as assisting his father.[15] Ambrose rose to a high position in York society, becoming one of the city chamberlains in 1674.[8] In 1676 he moved into a tenement (a disused chapel) on the southern corner of Common Hall Lane, the site now occupied by the Mansion House. The records of his tenancy show that he lived into the 18th century, at least until 1703.[57] The house remained with the Girdlers in occupation until John, son of Ambrose, died in 1716. Ambrose's change of parish from St Crux to St Martin le Grand is thus explained by his move to this tenement in Coney Street.

The youngest son Richard, born in 1634, received his father's "theorby lute" when John died in 1666.[24] Two manuscripts now in the British Library help prolong the history of Richard Girdler, but in tantalising incompleteness. Add. MS 33,595, some fragments of York history written in the mid 17th century, bears the signature of Richard Girdler dated "Anno Domi. 1655." Most is written by a single hand using brown ink, but post 1646 the writing changes to the same hand as signed the first page in black ink, that of Girdler. The likelihood of this being our Richard Girdler, fortunately an unusual name, is improved by the intelligence that the book was obtained in 1889 at a Sotheby's sale in Burton Constable, in East Yorkshire. However the fact must be faced that the hand of Richard Girdler, scribe, is not that of a boy of just twelve years.

"In regard of the extreame poverty of this citty"
Ambrose and Jane study the situations vacant columns

The second manuscript, Add. MSS 29,283-5 is a set of part books for instrumental trio by composers including Matthew Locke, Lully, Thomas Farmer, John Blow, John Hilton, and **Richard Girdler**. The books date from 1682 when the York Richard Girdler would have been a mature man of forty eight years. They were originally owned by one Thomas Fuller. He was not the well-known cleric Thomas Fuller, for he died in 1661. A chance mention of another Thomas Fuller in a letter from the current organist of Great St Mary's Church in Cambridge[55] mentions that a man of that name was appointed organist there in 1742; a long shot, but he may just have been the man. It is pleasant to fancy that Girdler had moved south as a musician among those great men in the London of Charles II and Samuel Pepys, but no more than the circumstances already described are offered as evidence. A thorough search by the principal reference librarian at the Guildhall Library in London revealed nothing about him.[20]

Another musician in the Girdler family was John's step-son William Webster who seemed destined for a waite's career, for John bequeathed him: "...all my winde instrementes...", but he died before taking up the post.[24] Jane had died in 1644 and John soon re-married (1645) this time to the twenty one year old widow of haberdasher Robert Webster. The unfortunate young William died shortly after his step-father and one wonders if it was the same illness which carried them both off. Both wills begin: "..., being sick and weake in body but of perfect mynde and remembrance".[24]

The Watson-Girdler pedigree has been determined to include eleven musicians, eight of whom were city waites. Although a son frequently took his father's profession, (see appendix I) in music as in any other trade, no York family was quite as all-musical until the mid 18th century when John Camidge returned from London to begin a hundred years of Camidge organists at the Minster.

THE WATSON-GIRDLER FAMILY PEDIGREE

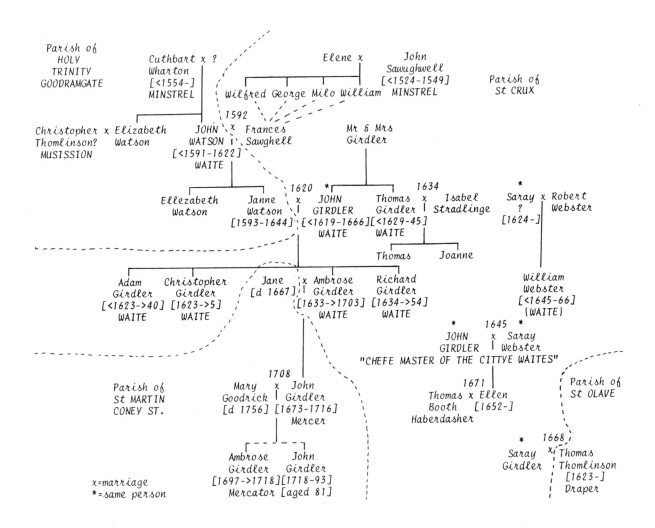

Parish of
HOLY
TRINITY
GOODRAMGATE

Parish of
St CRUX

Cuthbart x ?
Wharton
[<1554-]
MINSTREL

Elene x   John
              Sawughwell
              [<1524-1549]
Wilfred George Milo William MINSTREL

Christopher x Elizabeth
Thomlinson?   Watson
MUSISSION

JOHN   x Frances
WATSON   Sawghell
[<1591-1622]
WAITE

Mr & Mrs
Girdler

1592

Ellezabeth   Janne   x JOHN   Thomas x Isabel
Watson   Watson   GIRDLER   Girdler   Stradlinge
               [1593-1644] [<1619-1666][<1629-45]
                            WAITE   WAITE

1620 *   1634

*
Saray x Robert
?   Webster
[1624-]

Thomas   Joanne

Adam   Christopher   Jane   x Ambrose   Richard
Girdler   Girdler   [d 1667]   Girdler   Girdler
[<1623->40] [1623->5]   [1633->1703] [1634->54]
WAITE   WAITE   WAITE   WAITE

William
Webster
[<1645-66]
(WAITE)

*   1645 *
JOHN   x Saray
GIRDLER   Webster
"CHEFE MASTER OF THE CITTYE WAITES"

Parish of
St MARTIN
CONEY ST.

1708
Mary   x John
Goodrick   Girdler
[d 1756] [1673-1716]
           Mercer

1671
Thomas x Ellen
Booth   [1652-]
Haberdasher

Parish of
St OLAVE

* 1668
Saray   x Thomas
Girdler   Thomlinson
          [1623-]
          Draper

Ambrose   John
Girdler   Girdler
[1697->1718][1718-93]
Mercator [aged 81]

x=marriage
*=same person

The next generation of waites may have included those trained by the Girdlers: John Barehead and William Bridekirke, left by John Girdler "one trible violin" and "one little base viall" respectively.[24]

Then came the "band of Johns": John Sutton, John Edwards, John English, John Barehead, and John Storme. The sixth is not known but had he also been a John....! John Storme is a character to initiate interest for he originally gained his freedom as a "danceing master" in 1672,[8] then was appointed master waite in 1675.[15]

John Storme preparing a dance class, 1682

John Edwards has the rare distinction of being the only waite whose tomb has been located, but sadly it was destroyed by a bomb. His will was very explicit about the site of his burial:[24]

....in Saint Martins Church [Coney street] behinde the south doore neare to the steeple five foot deep at least and a marble slab to be laide upon my grave.

In his pamphlet "The Christmas Waits and Minstrels of Bygone York", 1909 the local antiquary TP Cooper confirms that Edwards had his last wish by quoting from the slab:[9]

Here lyeth ye body of John Edwards one of the waits of this city who dyed ye 9th Aug 1681.

The author has failed to locate Edwards's marble slab. The air raid of 29th April 1942 which all but destroyed the Guildhall, also did serious damage to the Church of St Martin le Grand. The incendiary bombs, or subsequent restoration of the church removed it completely but what's left of John Edwards, "five foot deep", should still be intact!

PART V - <u>THE EIGHTEENTH CENTURY</u> -

OBOES AND BASSOONS, VIOLINS AND VIOLONCELLOS

"At last bolted out from the corner of a street, a parcel of strange hobgoblins cover'd with long frize rugs and blankets, hoop'd round with leather girdes from their cruppers to their shoulders, and their noddles buttoned up into caps of martial figure, like a Knight Errant at tilt or tournament; one was armed, as I thought, with a lusty faggot-bat, and the rest with strange wooden weapons in their handes in the shape of Clyster-pipes, but as long, almost as speaking trumpets. Of a sudden they clap't them to their mouths and made such a frightful yelling, that I thought the world had been dissolving, and the terrible sound of the last trumpet to be within an inch of my ears. These are the City Waits, and have gowns, silver chains and sallaries, for playing Lilla Bolaro to my Lord Mayor's horse through the city".
                    Ned Ward, 1703

The waites' gallery in York Mansion House

Joseph Shaw (free, 1692)[8] may have been one of the waites disciplined by the council in October 1693[15] because of:

complaints made agst. the waites that they do not behave in their respective places as they ought to do.

How they misbehaved is not given (perhaps again they were "comon drunkerdes") but they were duly sacked and, as previously in 1566, ordered to turn in their badges and liveries to the Lord Mayor. The Chamberlains did not pay any waites for the next two years and again York was without its city band.

Shaw with his wife Ann lived in, or adjacent to St Andrewgate. The inventory of his belongings on his death in 1703 included amongst the contents of the kitchen:[24]

Here is another of those rare lists of a waite's instruments from which so much may be deduced of his, and by association, of his colleagues' musical activities. Cornetts had been part of the waites' outdoor band since roughly 1600, but they were to be replaced by oboes in the 18th century. Shaw had one of each and perhaps his career marks the period of change to the new sound of oboes and bassoons. Several previous waites had owned violins maybe used outdoors (see "York Waits" ballad above), but probably more useful for banquets and dances, along with the flutes. It is unfortunately not clear whether Shaw's flutes were of the transverse variety or the very popular recorders of the blossoming Baroque period.

William Tyreman or Tireman replaced Shaw in 1703. He came from a family in which the men were exclusively curriers and cordwainers. He is not mentioned in the freemens' roll at the time of his career as a waite but mysteriously appears in 1740, as an organist which indeed he was.[8] This promising young musician, "...sent to London for six months in order to improve him in the way of musick..."[15] was appointed organist of the parish church in Doncaster (St George's) in 1739 and moved on from there to Cambridge as organist at Trinity College in 1741. He matriculated as Bachelor of Music in 1757, and retired or died in 1777.[55] Not only did Tireman make a success of his musical career, but he became the richest of the York waites. The Gentleman's Magazine noted in its marriage column in 1746 that William Tireman, organist, married a Miss Browne of Doncaster....and a fortune of £20,000![14,44]

So far the city chamberlains' accounts have rarely mentioned to whom payment of the waites' salary was made. From 1717 onwards a name is given, presumably that of the chief waite. Thus, a payment of February 2nd, 1717 was written:[63]

To Mr English for his own and the use of the rest of the waites their years sallary due this day........0-8-4

Mr English was almost certainly Charles English (free, 1713) son of John English the waite.

1720 was the first year that payments were made to Mr Tireman (increased to £5-0-0). It would seem reasonable to presume that our William Tireman received the waites' wages until February 1741, after which he finally left Yorkshire to pursue his career in Cambridge. In the following four years (1742-5) payments passed to a Mr Buckley (Stephen Buckley senior?) but it is then that the Chamberlains' accounts of 1746-61 present the most tantalising puzzle in this musical history.[63] Once again it was "Mr Tireman" who took over. The Cambridge organist simply could not have acted on the behalf of the waites from so great a distance, and the records of Trinity College prove that he remained there until 1777.[55] So who was the second Mr Tireman? The explanation is being sought.

The first newspaper report to allude to the waites was in The Gazette and St. James Evening Post (London) in June 1727:[15]

They write from York that on Saturday evening upon receipt of the order of the Council and proclamation the Lord Mayor and aldermen attended by

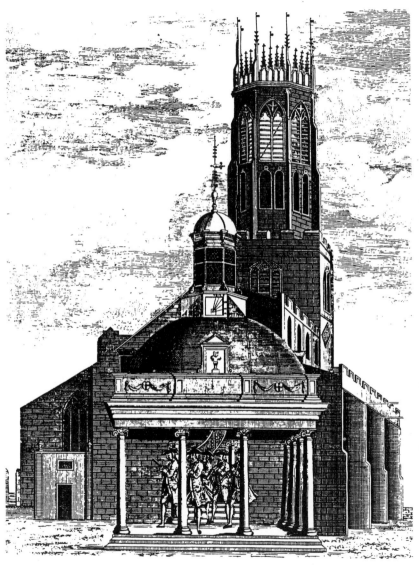

the whole body of the City in their gowns together with the clergy & principal Gentry with the same did immediately proceed from the Guildhall with Drums Trumpetts City Musick [the waites] & colours flying and proclaimed his Majesty King George the second in four quarters of the City [Guildhall Gates, Castlehill, Pavement Cross, and Minster Yard steps] the Lord Mayors Butler attending at each place with the City Gold Cupp where his Majesty's health was drunk under the discharge of the City

Pavement Cross

Gunns and the huzzas of several thousand people and afterwards the Lord Mayor returned to the Guildhall where the whole City and Gentlemen attending in procession were entertained at the City's expense and the populace with Hogsheads of ale at the bonefires and the night concluded with the most hearty expressions of loyalty could be uttered or contrived.

The event was even more remarkable in that it took place within two hours of news of the death of George I reaching York. The Archbishop was told just as he arrived home at his palace in Bishopthorpe, after a long journey. He begged leave of absence because he was so weary.[15]

Charles Pick (free, 1722)[8] was without doubt "one of ye citty waites" having been cited as such no fewer than seven times in the parish register of St Michael le Belfrey. He was the son of Oswald Picke, a waite of the 1680s, and with Mr Tireman, John Sydal, and two others would have been the "City Musick" playing in the accession celebrations. They also would have played in similar lavish procession, laid on for the announcement of the declaration of war against Spain in 1739.

This time we are told what instruments they played:[15]

....the procession began from the Guildhall preceeded by the City Waites with their Hautboys and Bassoons and four trumpetts....

General Barrell's regiment of Grenadiers, also in the procession, included in its ranks: "...several Officers with French Horns & Drums..." a splendid sight and sound.

Oboes were important in York music in the mid 18th century. Each year from 1733, for over forty years, the five waites were employed by the directors of the Assembly Rooms (built at that time) to play in the morning concerts and the evening assemblies during race week. Their contract stated that they would be paid:

half a guinea per man per night and one of them playing upon the Hautboy.

They also played violin but their complete band composition cannot be fully deduced. They certainly had their regular place at the assembly rooms, indeed the plans for the building (1732)[62] ordered that:

...a Gallery be built for the musick betwixt ye middle Collumns in ye Great Room next ye Recess and that the same be boss up by Iron Cramps....Barnard Dickinson to make a gallery for ye Waites in the Comon Assembly room...

They no longer had the exclusive right to musical employment and it seems that the ancient ordinance excluding "fforeyner" musicians (appendix V) was no longer observed for other local musicians were engaged for the entertainments in race week, and they came, not only from York, but from much further afield. Local players included a regular pair of oboe players James Blayclock and John Dixon, and the Beckwith family (Francis, Henry and George) with their colleague Thomas Thackeray (1737-53). Waites from other towns now played in York and these included those of Ripon, Leeds and Wakefield as well as a mysterious band known as "The four Skeldergate Waites" (1733 and 1736).[62] Now, Skeldergate is a street in the centre of York and a second lot of waites in this city was previously unthinkable, but they are recorded in a very matter-of-fact manner, and there is no reason to presume that any rivalry occurred. One wonders whether the three Beckwiths and Thackeray had previously been known by that name, an inference made from the sequence of entries in the Assembly Rooms account book.

This diversification of musical performance in the 18th century comes as no great surprise, for the concert as such had come into being in the London of Charles II as recorded in the diaries of Samuel Pepys. The waites' function as civic musicians was being supplemented with occasional concert performances, but their importance as the Lord Mayor's minstrels remained undiminished. Other musicians were professionals solely in concert music. Thus more music was to be heard in York in more varied types of performance, and later in the century the great music festivals began, at which time orchestras were made up of local players and imported professionals, many from London. The waites of the time also played.

In 1756 John Camidge was appointed organist of York Minster, successor to James Nares who had been promoted to the Chapel Royal at Windsor.[1,2,10,22,28] Camidge had himself been at the Chapel Royal, under the tuition of Dr Maurice Green and the great George Frederick Handel. What an influence Camidge must have had on the provincial York waites when he was

appointed to direct the city music on his return to his home town! The
waites of the time would have looked quite like the gentlemen seen escaping
from the Fishes Head in the Illustrated London News picture (Dec 28, 1901).
The four waites, with violin, drum, and 'cello are sneaking away without
paying their bill, whilst the landlord slily prepares to overcharge a
wealthy patron, unwittingly evening the score.

JOHN CAMIDGE.
ORGANIST OF YORK MINSTER FROM 1756 TO 1799.

John Camidge's great-grandson Thomas Simpson Camidge had in his possession a miniature portrait of the great man in the waites' scarlet livery. Knowledge of the whereabouts of this miniature has, so far, eluded the author but an illustration in The Musical Times of May 1st 1903 may be the same.[10] This black and white reproduction is of a portrait of Camidge on the lid of a snuff box, but it is impossible to be certain that the young man in the fashionable powdered periwig is wearing his scarlet coat.

The new leader of the City Music brought the works of Handel with him and York, though the Minster authorities objected at first to their rather secular nature, soon became a focus of Handel performance. The Great Yorkshire Festivals of 1791-1835 always included memorable performances of "Messiah" in the Minster. This tradition is still repeated annually and the author and a friend were treated to one of life's great moments when visiting the north choir on the Saturday just before Christmas 1985: a sudden full-scale rehearsal of the Hallelujah Chorus. Thank you, John Camidge, for that!

This Camidge began an illustrious line of York Minster organists, himself 1756-99, Matthew (son), 1799-1842, John II (grandson), 1842-58, and his great-grandsons, Thomas Simpson and John III were also organists in York and Beverley respectively.

If the Mr Tireman who accepted the waites' pay from 1746-61 was simply an accountant or the like, the next man to do so, Mr Thomas Shaw[63] was certainly a practising waite, being one of the five sworn into office in February 1770.[15] They were: Thomas James, Thomas Shaw the elder, James Watson, Thomas Shaw the younger, and John Barnard. The last, though a waite at the time, was employed by the Assembly Rooms as one of those additional musicians and must have "cleaned up" each race week. Of these men nothing further has been discovered, despite laborious attention to the lists of wills in the York register.[24] It had, of course, been hoped to discover a connection between the two Thomas Shaws and Joseph Shaw. Another Joseph Shaw, musician appears in the freemens' roll in 1765[11] but again no connection has been proven. The swearing of 1770 is the only time that the waites' oath is recorded:[15]

You shall be obedient to the Lord Mayor or his deputy for the time being and shall attend and play upon such musical instruments as you are best masters of in all services of the Corporation when required by him or his deputy - you shall attend the sheriffs of this City in their public Cavalcade [the sheriffs' riding of the city limits] to read the proclamation on or about Martinmas and also each sheriff on the day he makes an entertainment for the Lord Mayor and Aldermen [at the Black Swan, Coney Street, now demolished] for which service you shall receive from each sheriff one guinea but if the sheriffs or either of them require your further attendance for the entertainment of their friends paid as such services may deserve. You shall call the city [observe the morning watches] from the first Monday after Martinmas to the end of February that is every Monday Wednesday and Fryday.

For the employment of five waites a fifth chain was made. One wonders how the waites had managed since 1567, there having been five of them from 1592 until 1619 and up to six from then until about 1700 but only four chains.[15,26]

From 1775 until 1825 the waites salary was received without a break by Mr James Watson.[63] This represents a continuous career of fifty years, unless the scant information available disguises a father-son occupation. Only one James Watson is to be found in the roll of freemen (1781)[11] and we must at present tentatively conclude that this man had the longest career of all the York waites. A Mansion House account sheet, undated, but probably from 1814-15, shows us that James Watson may have been alive at the time, but was not at his best:

Minister and singers...4 @ 9/6
Band @ 10/4
Barnard 10d and as City Waits 3/-
Brown as Leader of City Waites 1/1
Watson & Kilvington as City Waites
but unable to perform from old age 10/6

A Perspective View of the inside of the Grand Assembly Room in Blake street YORK.

Published according to Act of Parliament November 1759.

York City Art Gallery

PART VI - *THE NINETEENTH CENTURY-*

THE LAST OF THE WAITES

"Your committee are of the opinion
that the waits may be dispensed
with, and they recommend that office
to be abolished".

York City Council
8th February, 1836

The last time active waites are mentioned in the city records is in a minute of 15th January 1829, six years before they were disbanded by the Municipal Corporations Reform Act in 1836:[15]

Daniel Hardman of York musician appte one of the City Waits with the usual Salary.

Edmund, "peruke (periwig) maker" and Ann Hardman of 12, New Bridge Street, York had two sons, both prominent in the city's musical life in the first decades of the 19th century. William Hardman (born 1792) was a viola player, playing at a festival in Westminster Abbey in 1834. He was leader of the band of York Choral Society and conducted the church band of St Martin in Coney Street.[28] For the dancing at the grand fancy dress ball at the opening of the Yorkshire Musical Festival in 1828 Hardman provided the music:

Over the entrance to the Egyptian Hall [previously called the great room] was erected an orchestra with flowers, evergreens, &tc. which was occupied by HARDMAN'S Quadrille Band.

....and Mr Hardman's quadrille band was put in requisition, to enable the dancers in the room to trip it on the light fantastic toe. We must say that celebrated (and justly so) as LITOLFF'S band is we could discover no inferiority in that of our fellow citizen.

His main occupation was the ownership of a music shop at 36, Coney Street, in the 18th century the property of the Knapton family. Not only did Hardman sell musical instruments and sheet music, but he was also a publisher, and a few of his publications are available for the interested reader in the "York

Music" box in the city library. The business was taken over by Mr Henry Banks on Hardman's tragic death in 1855. It was Hardman's habit to visit the Black Swan Hotel, and he set off as usual on 25th Nov 1855, but in the morning he was found:[28]

....huddled up and suspended of his neck to the Bannister at the foot of the stairs - dead.

The poor man had been deeply depressed by the death of his wife in April that year, and the York gossip about his condition and lack of interest in the shop had reached his ears. He could take no more.

Banks, Hardman's close assistant and natural sucessor, transferred the business to the site on the corner of Stonegate (formerly owned by Mr Ager, a grocer particularly well-known for his teas) where Banks' Music of York remained the foremost shop of its kind to the present. The business moved in 1985 to Lendal and the old premises were developed to increase the city's surfeit of pure new wool sweaters!

A biography of Daniel Hardman, the last of the York waites, is to be found in the manuscript: A list of York Musicians by J W Knowles, 1924:[26]

DANIEL HARDMAN became a member of the city waits whose title was also the city band Dr Camidge being the leader. At this period they wore a livery and had a silver badge on the sleeve of one arm and it was their custom to play at all civic gatherings and processions of the civic body also as City watch they perambulated the streets at night for four weeks counting from Martinmas and after playing a very quaint but catchy tune the leader called out the time of night and the state of the weather. In 1835 when the Municipal Corporations Act passed the Waits were abolished as official musicians and pensioned off with an annuity of £2:10 each.

Regrettably the works of Knowles (an admired glass painter) are frequently "imaginative" and there is no evidence that Dr Camidge (John Camidge junior) was leader of the city waites as his Grandfather truly had been.

About 1836 a series of concerts was given in Leeds and at the last a quartet by Haydn was performed, also a quintet for two violins, viola, and two 'cellos, D Hardman playing 'cello. A trio by Corelli, normally for two violins and 'cello was played on two 'cellos and double bass, the latter played by Mr Hardman:[26]

Much amusement was caused by the double bass player who was built somewhat in proportion to his huge instrument and wore a double curly wig which his energetic playing tended to displace. Before he was halfway through the jig in the Corelli trio it began to make a gradual journey round his head until at the finish of the movement the back of the wig rested on his forehead whilst the curls reposed gracefully on his coat collar.   [Knowles does not give the source]

......a double curly wig
which his energetic
playing tended to dislodge

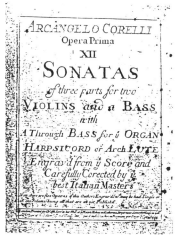

In the last three years all three waites were named in the chamberlains' accounts: Richard Brown, Christopher Brown, and Daniel Hardman.[59] In the orchestra for the Great Musical Festival in 1828 were the 'cellist "Hardman D" and the double bass players "Brown" and "Brown, jun", who must surely have been the three waites. It does strike one that such an ensemble would have made a bizarre city band! Such evidence makes it difficult to say quite what instruments the waites did play after the sparse records of oboes and bassoons come to an end. Certainly that Georgian band had become thoroughly outmoded by the 19th century, and the revolution of instrument design, led by Sax, Heckel, and Mr Wigglesworth of Otley had begun. We have already deduced, in the section of this book which deals with waites' instruments that Daniel Hardman was the player of some sort of up-to-date brass instrument, but what the Browns played is a total mystery. Our only hint comes from TP Cooper's drawing entitles "Coppergate 1809", in which the waites are playing violin, 'cello, ophicleide, and an unseen instrument. Did he know?

Hardman evidently had some idea that his career with the city council was coming to its end in 1835. He maintained his skill in the trade of his father, hairdressing, and took his freedom as such (not as a musician) in 1828.[11] In 1832 he continued the family hairdressing business at number 12, New Bridge Street and later that year extended to Oyster Rooms at the same address:[46]

OYSTER ROOMS,
12, *New Bridge Street, York.*
DANIEL HARDMAN begs to announce, that he has appropriated Rooms for the SALE of NATIVE MILTON OYSTERS, and is happy to be enabled to add, that he has made such arrangements in London as will ensure a regular supply DIRECT FROM THE VESSELS, by which he confidently hopes to secure them of the finest quality, and in the highest condition.
Oysters in Barrels sent to Order.

Ophicleide

Then in late 1833 he and James Walker formed their famous brass band, the first of two as illustated by an account of the General Election razzmatazz in 1835:

The two bands of music were also set to work, York for generations had a 'Blue Band' and an 'Orange Band.' Mr Bean was leader of the Blue Band, and the favourite tune of his company were 'Hurrah for the bonnets of blue,' 'Maggie Lauder,' 'Blue bonnets over the border' and such like. Mr Hardman, and afterwards Mr Walker, was the leader of the orange band, and the latter was decidedly a better musician and a more energetic man than the 'blue' bandmaster, but that did not go for much in those days.

Rivalry between the two bands was serious and were they to meet at a convenient street corner the contest would be continued, it is said, not without "blows and scrimages". Eventually in 1839 the Bean band issued a challenge to a musical duel for ten pounds per side, but the whole thing had to be postponed when the "energetic" Walker fell ill because of the strain and excitement of the build-up.

In July 1835 D Hardman, perhaps hurriedly, advertised in the Yorkshire Gazette that "he continues to give instruction on the violoncello and double bass".[47]

INSTRUCTION ON THE
VIOLONCELLO & DOUBLE BASS.
D. HARDMAN respectfully intimates that he continues to give Instruction on the above Instruments. Terms and further Particulars may be known on application at D. HARDMAN's 12, Bridge-street; or at HARDMAN's Music Warehouse, Coney-street.

York, July 2nd, 1835.

The council minute books tell the last part of the waites' story:

The number of City Waits was formerly five, but is now reduced to two, the vacancies occasioned by death not having been supplied. Mr Christopher Brown and Mr Daniel Hardman are the survivors. Their salaries are £4 per annum each, with Livery Coats and Hats found once in six years, the expense whereof has averaged £1:1:0 per annum each.

Your Committee are of the opinion that the Waits and the Tipstaves may be dispensed with, and they recommend those offices to be abolished.

8th February, 1836

Resolved....that bonds be given under the Common Seal to Mr Daniel Hardman and Mr Christopher Brown, late City Waits, for securing the payment of an Annuity of £2:13:4 to each of them, for his life, being compensations directed by the Lords of the Treasury to be paid to them respectively for the loss of their said office.

13th February, 1837

Despite his small annuity, bankruptcy was Hardman's fate in 1847, during the time that he was landlord of the Ebor Tavern in North Street. His goods were assigned into the hands of receivers, to be offered to his creditors.[48] This did not break Hardman for we learn a younger contemporary bandsman, Enderby Jackson of Hull, writing in 1896:[25]

Mr Dan Hardman, now over ninety years of age, is still living, and receives his yearly pension as the sole surviving member of the Ancient Order of the York City Waits...

Where Daniel Hardman spent his last years has not yet been discovered. Hugh Murray's "Pedigrees of York families" which deals with the Hardmans in some detail does not mention his death or burial, and the author's own efforts to find his will have been disappointing. One can only assume that he ended his days in the care of family or friends, a very elderly representative of York's distant past, and that having few posessions, he left no will......or that he is still alive. It is astonishing to note that he lived throughout the reign of Queen Victoria which included the beginning of the brand new system of local government that ended our friends the waites and forced him into a new life-style. He also saw the arrival of gas, then electric lighting, the hey-day and end of the stagecoach, the invention of photography, half the history of the steam railways, and the first motor cars. What a wise old man he would have been obliged to be. In all probability, someone, somewhere has a photograph of Daniel Hardman, the last of the York waites.

Afterthought

A grave stone in the churchyard of St Michael, Alnwick bears an insciption ideal for Daniel Hardman's last resting place:

This stone
was erected by friends
and admirers of
Thomas Coward
musician,
The last of the "Waits"
of this ancient borough
who died on the 6th. of Feb. 1845
aged 61 years.

Mute is the music. Motionless is the hand
That touched with "Magic bow" the trembling strings.
But memory hath embalm'd those Viol tones
Which fill'd the enraptured ear and charm'd the soul.

682   PUNCH, *or The London Charivari*   [December 19, 1934

Maid. "MR. SCROOEY DOESN'T BELIEVE IN WAITS."
Leader (grimly). "HE WILL BEFORE WE LEAVE."

PART VII - YORK'S OTHER MUSICIANS

"A poor fidler is in worse case than his fiddle. He is one that rubs two sticks together as the indians strike fire, and rubs a poore livinge from it. A good feast shall drawe him five miles by the nose and his other pilgrimages are fairs and good houses, where his devotion is great to the Christenmas: and no man loves good times better. He is in league with the tappsters for the worshipfull of the inn, whom he torments next morning with his art. A new songe is to him better than a new jacket, especially if bawdy, which he calls merry, and hates naturally the puritan, as an enemy to his mirth. A country weddinge, and Whitson-ale, are two main places he domineers in, and he goes for a musitian, and over-looks the bagpipe. The rest of him is drunk, and in the stocks".

Bishop John Earle, 17th C.

Of the 178 York musicians so far named (and listed in Appendix I), 66 have been identified as waites or probable waites. Of the remaining 112 less is known, for most records were made by the council about its own employees, ie the waites. These men were independent practitioners, but occasional council directives, disciplines, or wills provide fragmentary data.

After those named already as possible early waites in the 14th and 15th centuries the first man of with a story was John Sawghele. That particular spelling of his surname is the first, found in the roll of freemen in 1524.[7] His sons were spelt "Sawhell" in the same source; in his will he was "Sawughwell",[24] and his grand-daughter ffrances was spelt "Sawghell" in the parish register of Holy Trinity, Goodramgate, noting her marriage to John Watson the waite. Perhaps we may deduce that, on balance, the name was pronounced "Saw-gell". From his will it is clear that, like many York musicians, he also ran an inn. There seems to have been a reasonable number of such establishments in Fossgate where the Sawghell family lived at "the syne of the paicoke" (Peacock). His sons avoided both of their father's trades, and Wilfrid and William were tailors, George and Milo, Goldsmiths. His will names only his wife Elene and daughter Margaret. The others come under the simple term "all my childer".

The Bannester family first occurs with the freedom of John senior in 1536.[7] He was evidently a harper for he bequeathed his "boy" (apprentice) Edward Bannyster his "litle dubble harppe"[24] but nothing to his son John who succeded him as a musician for at the time he was sick and thought unlikely to outlive his father. His wife, Marryon, inherited the lease of the house in Walmgate and a cow for which John had provided 3s:4d, presumably to complete payment for it. The people of York kept their stock in and around their dwellings in the narrow streets. The large quantity of dung under foot was quite unpleasant, not to say unhealthy, and the council made several attempts to persuade them to move their animals outside the city walls, but to no avail. Stock were more secure at home, and the humm of rotting manure accompanied by the buzzing of flies remained as the sensory stimuli characteristic of the city. Long after his unexpected recovery, John junior was also an innkeeper who lost the license of his "alehouse or tipling house" in 1589 "after a great disorder by diverse disordred fidlers and others".[58]

It is a pity that so little of note was written of Cuthbert Watson for it was he whose son John was the first waite of the Watson-Girdler family. He was a musician, searcher for the guild, and trained several of the waites by apprenticeship.

The publication of the ordinances of the York guild of musicians in 1561 and 1578 made life hard for professional musicians not employed as city waites. John Sawghell had kept a respectable inn as a supplement to his income from music earlier in the century, but we have already seen John Bannester the younger discharged from keeping his disorderly alehouse in 1589. Other musicians also enfringed the law and it is evident that the waites had the lion's share of the available income from music and the others scrapped for the remainder. The reports of the quarter sessions etc give a picture of extreme competitiveness and territoriality amongst the non-waite musicians, and that was almost certainly associated with poverty and petty crime. Musicians were disciplined for three main categories of misdemeanour: infringement of the waites' privileges as set out in the ordinances; keeping illegal drinking and brewing establishments; and squabbling.[58]

Robert Collyer, fell foul of the law with great frequency, perhaps simply to avoid poverty. He set up an unlicenced inn and in 1579 was ordered not to brew or tipple ale, then in 1582 banned from keeping his inn. He encroached on waites territory in ca 1578 and in the following year had to be bound over to keep his peace with other musicians, namely Richard Harrison and William Sparke. Robert and Ellen Collyer lived in a tenement on Foss Bridge.

Robert Collyer died in 1591. Robert Sympson was, according to available records, a man of contrasts. In 1599 and 1606 he was one of the two searchers of the guild of musicians, presumably a post of some responsibility. He was also frequently in trouble, like his contemporaries already cited, for playing in contravention of the ordinances, with strangers, or with the like of Cuthbert Thompson and John Clerke, ex-waites, when they muscled in on the Hunts Up scene...and got caught.

The families Laverock and Pacock in their diverse spellings appear frequently and usually respectably. Father, son, and grandson Laveroke (Richard, Christopher, and Thomas) were all musicians from 1578-1628. Thomas Laverock was apprenticed to John Yonge one of the two musician sons of waite William Yonge (1615). Richard Laverock and Robert Pacock were both, in their time, searchers for the guild, but whereas the Laverock family always seems to have been at least comfortable, Pacock was cited in 1611 to be a "poor man" and given leave to keep an alehouse.[55]

John Peirson and John Storme became enfranchised freemen in 1672, the two earliest dancing masters in the history of York[8] (dancing really took off with the opening of the Assembly Rooms in the early 1730s). In 1651 John Playford marked the increasing popularity of the English country dance with the publication of his "The English Dancing Master", a substantial collection of popular tunes with instruction for dancing such as "Cuckolds all arow", "The punk's delight", and "Parsons farewell".[4,36] It may well be that these new printed editions had become popular in York by the time these two men embarked on this new career, but sadly nothing is yet known of dancing in York before the splendid Georgian balls for which the assembly rooms became a focus in the following century.

Of William Wood (free 1651) nothing is known yet one relic survives: in print (Francis Drake, 1736,[12] TP Cooper[9] 1909, and various books on coin collecting) and in museums and collections. Wood published a trading token, a fashion of the 17th century arising out of a need for small change and upon its face is the inscription: WILL:WOOD.IN.YORK.MVTISIO*HIS HALF PENNY. It will be noticed that the abbreviation of "Musitian" is mis-spelt, the "s" and "t" being transposed. No significance is suggested.

The Punchenello on the obverse suggests that Wood was more than just a musician, but perhaps an all-round entertainer with music, song, puppetry, or even conjuring in his repertoire.

The naming of John Camidge in this work leads one on to the many eminent musicians who were organists of York Minster and, of course, his family. For the former the reader is referred to the plentiful literature on the subject of the Minster.[1,2] For the latter; well the Camidge family history has yet to be fully researched by his descendants, but it should prove well worthwhile. The grandson, Dr John Camidge, was a friend of William Etty the painter, and features in Etty's detailed and sensitive correspondence. Behind the Statue of Etty in Exhibition Square, on the façade of York art gallery, are four carved faces, one of which is Dr Camidge! It has been reported[44] that the Camidge family entertained Mendelssohn and Dickens as house-guests.

Thomas Haxby free 1758[11] was a local manufacturer of keyboard instruments. His biography by his descendant David Haxby is published in The York Historian.[19] A good number of his instruments survive today and some are playable. A square forte-piano by Haxby, owned by the York Castle Museum is occasionally set up for performances but, if one is to judge from a recording of this instrument, it does not appear to respond well to tuning.

The music retail business at 36, Coney Street, once run by William Hardman (now Banks Music Ltd.) was previously owned by the Knapton family, Samuel (1756-1831), a 'cellist, known affectionately as "the father of the Musical Society", and his son Philip (1788-1833), joint director of the grand Minster Messiahs with Dr John Camidge and William Greatorex, organist of Westminster Abbey. A rather touching confession in the Musical Society's minutes shows that one of the committee in 1855 had pinched some pictures:[64]

I admit that the portraits of Dr Camidge's grandfather, of Mr Knapton, and of Mr John Brook, now in my house [The York Tavern] are the property of the York Musical Society.

signed C Harker

It is quite clear that in the late 18th and early 19th centuries several York families were involved in all sorts of music-making together, and that they probably knew each other well, though at different social levels. The Hardmans were the ordinary performers and providers of musical services, Daniel the waite and William the shopkeeper and dance-band leader. They both played in festival orchestras directed by a Camidge and a Knapton (shopkeeper, made good). At the top, the Camidges were Minster organists with one of the most important musical posts in the nation. It was the Camidges and Knaptons whose portraits were painted, not the Hardmans, whose lives ended with tragedy and poverty.

Only James Scruton remains for a brief mention, brief because little is known of him but that he was an oboe player (free 1809)[11] who played in the festival orchestras, originally as a York man and later from Liverpool. Presumably he moved house.

FINALE

Almost the last musicians for consideration were those few brave
souls who annually revived the tradition of winter musical watches,
TP Cooper's "Christmas waits of bygone York".[9] Perhaps it was they who
stimulated an exasperated poet in Punch (Dec. 1842) to pen the following:

A SONG OF THE NIGHT.

BY A SUFFERER.

AIR.—" Obvious."

WHAT un-fairylike music
  Steals slumber from me?
Provoking a sentence
  That beginneth with D!
'Tis the voice of the trombone,
  Blown with might and with main,
As it mingles its tone
  With the shrill cornet's strain.

The cabs are all hushed,
  And the busses at rest:
But these sleep-murd'ring wretches
  The still streets infest.
My ears from their torments
  No night-cap can save:
So I groan for the summons
  To get up and shave.

Leaping ahead to the 1970s we find the early music revival beginning in York. From the University the bug spread to a large number of musicians already inspired by the work of the late David Munrow, and amateur groups sprang up all over the place with various names such as **Kemp's Consort**, **The Aire Consort**, **The Medieval Street Band**, **In Nomine**, and **The York Waits** concealing the fact that the same people were trying different combinations of personnel and instrumentation. The last of those groups had a concrete raison d'être, the performance of ancient popular music as it would have been presented to the citizens of York in bygone times. It was a winning formula and the band has survived since those early efforts of 1977 with little change other than a constantly-improving presentation.

It was the author's involvement with **The York Waits** which inspired the desire to know more of the original waites. It is possible to have a good idea of the sounds of the old waites from the recordings made by today's band. However it is hoped that, in the near future, music selected especially to accompany this book will be recorded so that the reader may read the history of the waites, see their likenesses, and also hear their sounds, at leisure.

THE END

"This Pyllor Made The Meynstrels"

A pillar decoration in St. Mary's Church, Beverley. This sculpture depicting
five musicians with - left to right - pipe & tabor, viol, alto/tenor shawm,
cittern/lute, and soprano shawm, was given by the Beverley musicians' guild
in about 1524. These liveried musicians, with chains of office about their
necks, must surely be the Beverley waites. Illustrations of waites from any
period are in very short supply, indeed virtually non-existent, so that this
sculpture of Tudor waites in Yorkshire is of inestimable value to this book.

APPENDIX I

The musicians of York listed chronologically as in the roll of freemen.
Where the name is bracketed it does not occur in the roll of freemen but
the musician is first known in an alternative source at the given date.

WAITE=certainly a waite
waite=probably a waite

1304	THOMAS LE WAYTE		wayte
1319	WILLELMUS DE BURGH	harper	
1340	WILLEMUS DE LYNCOLN	piper	
1343	ADCIIS DE YORKOSAY (sic)	organista	
1349	JOHANNES DE ROTHERHAM	organista	
1363	ROGERUS WAYTE	piper	waite
1365	JOHANNES DE TOPPCLYF	harpmaker	
1373	WILLELMUS DE CAYTON	piper	
1391	JOHANNES DE STYLLINGTON	piper	
1393	WILLELMUS DE LANGETON	mynstrall	
1394	NICHOLAS DE BLACKBURN	mynstrell	
1435	JOHANNES SEYMOUR	organ maker	
1440	JOHANNES SHENE	mynstrall	WATE
1453	(ROBERTO CLOSSE)		WAITE
1472	WALTERUS KIRKBY	mynstrall	
1475	JOHANNES SWYNBOURNE	mynstrall	
1475	EDWARDUS BOYSE	orgonmaker	
1483	EDW. SKERNE	mynstrell	
	[ ] SHENE	mynstrell	waite
1485	INNAS BINAN	orgoner	

1486	ROBERTUS LEMYNGTON	mynstrell	waite
	ROBERTUS COMYLTON	mynstrell	WAITE
	WILLELMUS PLOMBRE	mynstrell	waite
1487	JOHANNES HUGH	orgonmaker	
1493	RICARDUS TWYSDAY	mynstrall et brewer	
1498	NICHOLAS BELL	mynstrall	
1502	XPOFFERUS LOWE	mynstrall	
1503	ROGERUS SMALWODE	mynstrell	WAITE
1506	JOHANNES SYMSON	mynstrall	
1507	ROBERTUS MARSHALL	mynstrall	
1511	EDWARDUS GREWARD	mynstrall	
1514	JOHANNES HARPER	mynstrall	WAITE
1520	THOMAS SUTHERTON	mynstrell	
	THOMAS CUNSBY	mynstrell	
1524	JOHANNES SAWGHELE	mynstrell	
1533	WILLELMUS HYLL	mynstrell	WAITE
1536	JOHANNES BANESTER	mynstrell	
1541	HENRICUS KNYGHT	wayte	WAITE
1546	NICHOLAS WRIGHT	mynstrell	WAITE
1547	RICARDUS HARPER	mynstrell	
1553	WILLELMUS BROWNE	mynstrell	
	CUTHBART WHARTON	mynstrell	
	ROBERTUS SPARKE	mynstrell	
1554	JOHANNES BANYSTER	mynstrell	
	(son of Johannis Banester de Ebor mynstrell)		
	THOMAS DAVYSON	mynstrell	
1558	ROBERTUS HUSTHWATE	mynstrell	WAITE
	THOMAS MOWAR	mynstrell	WAITE
1560	(ROBERT BRADLEY)	musician	
1561	AMBROSE BURGH	harper	
1561	ARTHUR HODSHON	mynstrell	WAITE
1565	JOHN BAWDERSTONE	waite	WAITE

1569	RICHARD HARRISON	mynstrell	
1571	ROBERT COLLYER	musycon	
1572	JOHN CLERKE	mynstrell	WAITE
1575	THOMAS DALE	mynstrell	
1576	LAURENCE BARRON	mynstrell	
	WILLIAM SPARKE	mynstrell	
1578	RICHARD LAVEROCK	mynstrell	
1579	RICHARD BROWNE	mynstrell	
1580	(HENRIE SQUIER)		WAITE
1581	WILLIAM YONGE	mynstrell	WAITE
1584	PETER RUTLES	musyssion	
1585	JOHN WILSON	mynstrill	
	WILLIAM JOHNSON	mynstrill	WAITE
	CHRISTOFER DENT	mynstrill	WAITE
1587	THOMAS GRAVE	mynstrill	WAITE
1591	JOHN WATSON	musission	WAITE
	(son of Cuthbart Watson)		
1595	JOHN HARRISON	mynstrill	
	(son of Richard Harrison)		
1596	ROBERT PACOKE	musission	
	CUTHBERT THOMPSON	musission	WAITE
1600	RICHARD BRADLEY	mussission	WAITE
1603	MARCUS COWPER	mussission	
1603	(JOHN BRADLEY)		WAITE
	(nephew of Richard Bradley)		
1604	CHRISTOPHER THOMPSON	mussission	WAITE
	JOHN BARTON	mussission	
	GEORGE ATKYNSON	mussission	
	CHRISTOPHER THOMLYNSON	mussission	
	WILLIAM CLERKE	mussission	
	(son of John Clerke)		

1605	CHRISTOPHER LAVEROKE	mussission	
	(son of Richard Laveroke)		
1608	STEPHEN BRITTEN	Organbuilder	
1609	THOMAS YONGE	mynstrill	
	(son of Wm. Yonge)		
1611	JOHN BENSON	musition	
1612	JAMES SIMPSON	musition	
	JOHN WILSON	musition	
	(son of John Wilson)		
	SIMON HOLMES	musition	
1615	JOHN YONGE	musicion	
	(son of Wm. Yonge)		
1616	RALF KIDD	musition	WAITE
1619	JOHN GIRDLER	musitioner	CHEFE WAITE
1621	CHRISTOPHER SETLE	musiconer	
1623	PATRICK HOWELL	musiconer	
1624	ROBERT BLACKBURNE	musiconer	
1625	RICHARD WARD	musiconer	waite
1626	JOHN PICKERING	musiconer	
1628	THOMAS LAVEROCK	musiconer	
	(son of Christopher Laverock)		
1629	THOMAS GIRDLER	waite	WAITE
	(brother of John Girdler)		
ca 1630	EDWARD MILLINGTON	city trumpeter	
1632	MARK SPARKES	musiconer	
1633	ROBERT BARKER	musitian	
1637	RICHARD THOMPSON	musitian	WAITE
	(son of Christopher Thompson)		
1638	ADAM GIRDLER	musitian	WAITE
	(son of John Girdler)		
1640	WILLIAM SEWELL	musitian	
1651	WILLIAM WOOD	musitioner	

1654	CHRISTOPHER GIRDLER (son of John Girdler)	musitioner	WAITE
	AMBROSE GIRDLER (son of John Girdler)	musitioner	waite
	RICHARD GIRDLER (son of John Girdler)	musitioner	waite
	JOHN HOLMES (son of Symon Holmes)	musitioner	
1661	THOMAS KADE	musitioner	
1664	GEORGE TOLLETT	musitioner	
	WILLIAM WEBSTER	musitioner	(waite)
1666	JOHN BAREHEAD	musition	WAITE
1667	WILLIAM PAGET	musition	
	JOHN SUTTON	musition	
	SAMUEL BATEMAN	musition	
	JOHN EDWARD	musition	WAITE
	(JOHN ENGLISH)	not listed	waite
1672	THOMAS CAREY	musiconer	
1672	JOHN PEIRSON	dancinge master	
	JOHN STORME	dancinge master	WAITE
1676	HENRY HODGESON	musicon	
1689	NATHAN HARRISON	musition	WAITE
1680	OSWOULD PICKE	musition	WAITE
1692	THOMAS CADE (son of Thos. Cade)	(musician)	
	JOSEPH SHAW	musitian	WAITE
1703	WILLIAM CAREY (son of Thos. Carey)	(musician)	
1705	WILLIAM PICK (son of Oswald Pick)	(musician)	
1710	NATHAN HARRISON (son of Nathan Harrison)	(musician)	

1713	CHARLES ENGLISH	(musician)	WAITE
	(son of John English)		
	JOHN STORM	musitioner	
	(son of John Storme)		
1717	(STEPHEN BULKLEY)		WAITE
1722	CHARLES PICK	musitian	WAITE
	(son of Oswald Pick)		
1723	(JOHN SYDAL)		WAITE
1733	THOMAS FLEMING	musitian	
	(FRANCIS BECKWITH)		
	(HENRY BECKWITH)		
	(GEORGE BECKWITH)		
	(THOMAS THACKERAY)		
1735	(JOHN DIXON)	oboe player	
1737	(JAMES BLAYCLOCK)	oboe player	
1740	WILLIAM TIREMAN	organist	WAIT
1742	([ ]BUCKLEY)		WAITE
	(DAN WHALLEY	oboe player	
	(JOHN PRIESTLEY)	violinist	
1746	(STEPHEN BUCKLEY)		WAITE
	(Son of [ ] Buckley)		WAITE
1750	(THOMAS SEDGEWICK)	violinist	
	(WILLIAM SHAW)	violinist	
	(GEORGE HARRISON)		
1753	(HENRY MIDDLETON)		
1754	THOMAS JENKINS	musition	
1756	THOMAS JAMES	musician	WAITE
	(THOMAS SHAW Snr)		WAITE
	(THOMAS SHAW Jnr)		WAITE
ca 1756	(JOHN CAMIDGE Snr)		(WAITE)
1758	THOMAS HAXBY	musical instrument maker	
	THOMAS KEAY	musicon	WAITE

1765	JOSEPH SHAW	musician	WAITE
1766	(Wm HUDSON)		WAITE
1767	JOHN BARNARD	musician	WAITE
	([ ] HALFIELD)		
1774	THOMAS THACKRAY	musician	
	WILLIAM AUDESLEY		
1778	JOHN HAXBY	musical instrument maker	
1782	JAMES WATSON	musician	WAITE
1793	THOMAS KILVINGTON	musician	WAITE
1999	HENRY BARNARD	musician	
1800	RICHARD COLLINGWORTH	music master	
1809	JAMES SCRUTON	musician (oboe player)	
1820	CHRISTOPHER BROWN	musician	WAITE
1826	WILLIAM DUTTON	musician	
1827	(RICHARD BROWN)		WAITE
	(probably senior of C Brown)		
1828	DANIEL HARDMAN	hairdresser	WAITE
	(WILLIAM HARDMAN)	(musician)	
1829	JOHN TOMLINSON	professor of music	
	THOMAS HAXBY TOMLINSON	professor of music	
1830	WILLIAM BOLTON jun	musician	
	SAMUEL COLLIER	musician	
	CHARLES HARGITT	teacher of music	
	JAMES MARSH	musician (piano resaler)	

APPENDIX II

A chronological list of instruments in York Literature

Source Code: F=*Roll Of Freemen*
W=*Will*
H=*Corporation House Books*
C=*City Chamberlains' Accounts*
M=*York Minster Accounts*
A=*Assembly Rooms records*
N=*The Gazette & St James Evening Post*
G=*Yorkshire Gazette*
Y=*York Courant*
MFP=*Musical Festival Programme*
P=*Poem*
EJ=*Enderby Jackson, 1896*

Year	Instrument	Source
1319	Harp, William de Burgh ("harper")	F
1343	Woodwind, William de Lyncoln ("piper")	F
1349	Organ? John de Rotherham ("organista")	F
1363	Woodwind, Roger Wayte ("piper")	F
1373	ditto William de Cayton	F
1391	ditto John de Styllington	F
1446	Fiddle ("fiddler")	C
1446-7	Trumpet ("Trumpetters")	C
1447&8	Lute? ("Hugo Luter")	C
1447&9	Lute ("lutanist")	C

1539   Shawm, John Harper (waite). ("a noys of pipes
       called shawmes")   W
1541   Trumpet, "the Trumpytour" at the visit of Henry VIII   H
1558   Harp, John Bannyster ("a lytle dubble harppe")   W
1558   Shawm, William Hill (waite). ("a lowde trible pipe")   W
1558   Recorder/flute, William Hill. ("a sharpe
       quatrible pipe for the sill noyse")   W
1558   Bagpipe, William Hill ("my best baggepipe")   W
1561   Shawm, Nicholas Wright purchased a "base shalme"
       for eleven shillings   H
1561   Harp, Ambrose Burgh ("harper")   F
1565   Shawm, Thomas Mower (waite). ("a shawme in
       a case of ledder")   H
1566   Shawm, (waites). ("a noyse of 4 shalmes")   H
1584-7 Fife, John Balderston (waite).   C
1584-97 Drum, Edmund Archer, city drummer   C
1584   Trumpet   C
1591   Sagbuttes & Cornettes, York Minster (prob. the waites) M
1597   Trumpet, Edward Millington, city trumpeter
       frequently mentioned until his death in 1644   C&H
1602   Curtal, John Watson (waite). Lent £4 to puchase a
       "doble curtall or howboy"   H&C
1603   Trumpet, ("my Lord Dudley's trumpittes")   H
1603   Sagbut, (for the waites) purchased from Sir Major
       Vavasor for £8, and in the hands of John Watson   C&H
1622   Sackbut, John Girdler (waite)   H
1623   Cornett, Richard Bradley (waite). ("treble cornett")   W
1623   Viol, ditto, ("bass viall")   W
1630   Cornetts, (waites). Return of Lord President to York   H
1633   Trumpetts   H
1633   Cornettes, (prob. the waites). Visit of Charles I.   H
1634   Bagpipe, John Bartendale unsuccessfully hanged at York P

1639	Cornettes, (waites). Visit of Charles I ("their cornettes and ther lowd instrumentes")	H
1645	Cornetts, Sackbut, Shawm, Lizard, Recorders, Violin, Tenor Violin, Bandora, & Kit, Thomas Girdler (waite)	W
1665	Trumpet, ("my Lord ffretchwille Trumpette")	C
1666	Wind instruments, John Girdler (waite). ("all my winde instrementes")	W
	Viol, John Girdler (waite). ("one little base viall")	W
	Violin, John Girdler (waite). ("one treble violin")	W
	Theorbo, John Girdler (waite). ("one theorby lute")	W
1672	Drums and Trumpets	C
1675	Cornett, John Storme (waite)	H
1676	Trumpet, John Mortis ("my Lord ffretchwell Trumpeter, a ffrenchman") par. reg., St Martin Coney St	
ca 1700	Cornett)	
	Violin ("fiddle")) Broadside:	
	Curtal ("curtel"))"York Waits"	
	Theorbo ("theorbe")) by Mr Durden	
	Kit)	
1702	Drummers & Trumpets (proclamation of Queen Anne)	C
1703	Violin(2), Joseph Shaw (waite)	W
1703	Flute(2), Joseph Shaw (waite)	W
	Oboe(1), Joseph Shaw (waite). ("hautboy")	W
	Cornett(1), Joseph Shaw (waite)	W
1704	Violin, Charles Barnard, the blind boy to receive a fiddle at the city's charge	H
1704	Violin, Mary Salmon's blind boy to receive a fiddle	H
1727	Drums and Trumpets, (accession of George II)	N&H
1734-9	Trumpets	
1735-6	Oboe ("Hautboy" Mssrs Blayclock and Dixon and one of the waites)	A
1736	Violins (waites)	A

1739	Oboes, (waites). ("hautboys")	H
1739	Bassoons, (waites)	H
1739	French Horns and Drums,(General Barrell's Officers)	H
1740	Tumpets(4)	C
1741-70	Trumpets	C
1741	Violin &ct. (Wakefield waites)	A
1742	Violin (John Priestley)	A
1749	Drums	C
1751	Violin (Thomas Sedgewick William Shaw)	A
1753	Violin (William Shaw)	A
1773	Drum and Trumpet	C
1774	Drums and Trumpets	C
1780	Drum and Trumpet	C
1781)		
1785)	Drum, Trumpet, and French Horn	C
1786)		
1790	Drums and Trumpets	C
1823	Double Bass, Brown and Brown jun. (waites)	MFP
1828	ditto	MFP
1828	Violoncello, Daniel Hardman (waite)	MFP
1833	Trumpet, (probably valved) James Walker	EJ
1833	Brass instrument, Daniel Hardman	EJ
1835	ditto	MFP
1835	Violoncello, Pottage (waites revivalist)	MFP
1835	Violoncello, Daniel Hardman (waite)	G
1835	Double Bass, Daniel Hardman (waite)	G

APPENDIX III

Processions and Pageantry for Royal visitations and the other civic Splendours of York.

1448   HENRY VI

"....Henry the sixth was a pilgrim (at the shrine) of William on the vigil of Matthew. While the choir glorified he gave praise to Peter". After visiting shrines at Durham, Ripon, Bridlington, and Beverley he returned to York to celebrate the feast of the translation of Edward. There is no evidence that John Shene and two colleagues, the waites, were on duty that day.

1478   EDWARD IV

The city entertained the king and his huge retinue of nobles and their ladies at the end of September 1478. The king brought his four minstrels with him and the city paid them 6s.8d. The city waites were not mentioned in connection with the visit but the chamberlains' account of their annual wages notes their "....attending and being with the mayor...." implying that John Shene, Walter Kirkeby, and John Swynbourne were present in the civic party.

1483   RICHARD III

A good friend of York, Richard Plantagenet had homes at the castles of Middleham and Sheriff Hutton. During his short reign he made one state visit to the city and was received in great splendour by the newly-liveried corporation in streets hung with tapestries and lined with pageants. No record exists to show that the waites or any other musicians were present.

1486   HENRY VII

Richard was slain at the battle of Bosworth in 1485 and his Lancastrian rival Henry acceded to the throne. York would not have been an ideal place to visit but he did, with his new queen, Elizabeth of York in the spring of 1486. The city put on a show every bit as lavish as that produced for Richard but cleverly designed not to cause political offence to the new king. The red and white roses of the houses of Lancaster and York were combined in a mechanical display at Micklegate Bar as the king rode into the city:

"....craftelye conceyvid a place in maner of A heven of grete Ioy and Anglicall Armony (angelic harmony). vnder the heven shalbe a world desolaite full of treys and floures In the which shall spryng vp A rioall rich rede rose (Henry) convaide by viace (a device) vnto the which Rose shall appeyre an other Rich white rose (Elizabeth) vnto whome so being to gedre (together) all other floures shall lowte (bow) and evidently yeue suffrantie (give soreignty) shewing the Rose tobe principall of all floures...."

Somewhere in this or one of the numerous shows lining Micklegate the three waites may have played their part.

1541   HENRY VIII

To please the reputedly bad-tempered king Henry York decided to begin the welcome with grovelling at Fulford Cross:

"....& Therupon my sayd lorde mayre & hys Brederin felle downe of ther kneys and the sayd master Recorder then of hys kneys mayde a goodly proposycion of Submissyon vn to hys hyghnes as hereafter apperyth verbatim &c....we your humble Subiectes of your said City of yorke....haue agaynst our naturall allegyaunce disobedyently and contrary your grace ys lawes....greuously heynously and traitoryously offendyd your high invyncible and moste Royall maiesty...." Were the waites present for the welcoming show which followed? They would probably have been' William Hill, Henry Knyght, and one other playing John Harper's "noys of shawmes" but there is no evidence other than that they were in the employ of their Lord Mayor. One musician was certainly there, the king's trumpeter who "blew the Trump at ye tyme of the makyng of the proclamacion for the kyng".

1584   MYDSOMER EVEN

Each parish within the city kept a stock of armour to be worn by the male parishioners at times of strife and on midsummer eve a grand procession would be mounted in order that the council might ensure that the armour had been well maintained. The accounts for 1584 contain so much detail of the arrangements for that year's show that the procession may be described: During the two days leading up to the show of armour John Balderston the waite, accompanied by Edmund Archer, a drummer, paraded about the city playing his fife and warning the citizens to prepare for the event. On the day the procession was led by several "fforerydinge Champions", horse-riders dressed to represent sundry heroes. Following them came the city standard, the "Ancyant", flanked by two sword players enthusiastically waving their

charges about their heads. Indeed so flamboyant were their efforts that one
of them nicked a tear in the flag. One shilling was the cost of
"....mendinge of our Ancyant which one of the two hand sworde players
vnadvysedly rented". The ceremonial music was supplied by the city
trumpeter, two drummers, and the four waites, Robert Hewet, John Balderston,
John Clerke, and George Cowper. All but Cowper had been waites since the
recorded shawm days and it seems quite likely that shawms were their
instruments, indeed they may still have been using the old "noyse". Hundreds
of armed citizens would have followed behind, wearing corselets and helmets
and toting halberds or guns, parish by parish led by their constables.

1603   JAMES I & VI

Queen Elizabeth never visited York although plans were begun in 1575. Her
sucessor's grand arrival and the waites of the time have been discussed in
the main text of this work but "The True Narration" describing the event is
here quoted in full. It serves as a description of York's royal welcomes of
the 17th century:

"On Saterday being the sixteenth of Aprill, his Maiestie removed from
maister Inglesbye towards Yorke, being sixteene miles from Topcliffe: and
when he came about some three miles from Yorke, (the liberties of the Citie
extending so farre) maister Bucke and maister Robinson, Sheriffes of the
Citie met him, & with humble dutie presented him with their white staues:
which his Maiestie receiuing, hee deliuered them instantly againe, so they
attended him towards the Citie; within a mile of which, when his Highnesse
approached, there mette him the Lorde Burleigh, Lorde President of the
North, with many worthy Knights and Gentlemen of the shyre. These also
attended his person to Yorke. Where, when he came neare vnto the Citie,
there met him three of the Sergeants at Armes, late seruants to the deceased
Queene, who deliuered up their Maces which his Maiestie with Royall

curtesie, redeliuered to them, commaunding them to waite on him in their olde places, which presently they did. And at the same time the Sergeant Trumpeter, with some other of his fellows, did in like maner submit themselues, and render their seruice, which he beningly accepted, & and commanded them in like maner to waite on him.

Then rode he on till he came to one of the gates of Yorke; where the Lord Mayor of the Citie, the Aldermen, and the wealthiest Commoners, with abundance of other people met him. There a long Oration being made, the Lord Mayor deliuered the Sword and Keyes to his Maiestie, together with a Cup of Gold, filled full of Gold, which present his Maiestie gratefully accepted, deliuering the Keyes againe to the Lord Mayor; but about the bearing of the Sword there was some small contention, the Lorde President taking it for his place, the Lorde Mayor of the Citie esteeming it his. But to decide the doubt, the Kings Maiestie merily demaunded, If the Sword beeing his, they would not be pleased, that he should haue the disposing thereof. Wherevnto when they humbly answered, it was all in his pleasure, his Highnesse deliuered the Sword to one, that knew wel how to vse a sword, hauing been tryed both at Sea and on Shoare, the thrise honoured Earle of Cumberland, who bare it before his Maiestie; ryding in great state from the gate to the Minster. In which way there was a Conduit that all the day long ran white and claret wine, euery man to drinke as much as he listed.

From the Minster his Maiestie went on foote to his owne house, being the mannor of saint Maries, hauing all the way a rich Canopie ouer his head, supported by foure Knights, and being brought thither he was honourably receiued by the Lorde Burleigh, who gaue cheerfull entertainment to all the followers of his Maiestie during the time of his continuance in Yorke."

The five waites who played cornetts, saggbuts and curtal on the day at Micklegate and Bootham Bars have already been described in the text.

1617   JAMES I & VI

On King James's second visit to York there was again a row about who should carry a sword, this time the king's sword and those who argued were the Lord Chamberlain and the Earl of Cumberland. The King was asked to intervene and he judged that the latter should carry it as far as the city gates where he would exchange it for the city's sword. The house books record that: "....vpon the gaites of the said Cittie, ther were Trumpiters and waites sounding and playing...." much in the way that they had done fifteen years previously. They may have been John Watson, Richard Bradley, John Bradley, Edward Easton and two more, for there were by now six of them.

1633   CHARLES I

"And now it is orderd that there be Trumpeterrs on the out syde of Micklegatebarr yf they can be gotten and cornettes on the insyde to sound at his Maiesties entrance into the Cittye" was the order of the council in May 1633. After the king's visit on the 19th May it was minuted "....the waites sounding and playing on their Cornettes on both sydes of the gaite....". Presumably no trumpeters, not even Edward Millington, were available. The six Waites would certainly have been led by John Girdler, perhaps including Thomas Girdler and Richard Ward.

1639   CHARLES I

The arrangements for Charles the first's return visit were much the same as previously: "And that the waytes of this Cittie play upon Micklegate barr and on Bowthombarr....and if need bee that their Cognizances bee new burnished....the waytes of the Cittie were sounding and playing on their Cornettes and ther lowd instruments". Again John Girdler would have been in charge but the other waites cannot be determined.

1702   PROCLAMATION OF QUEEN ANNE

For the proclamation of the new Monarch the celebration included contributions from the city waites, trumpeters and drummers. Respectively they received 10 shillings, 7s.6d, and 5 shillings extra salary.

1727   THE ACCESSION OF GEORGE II

Within two hours of news of the death of George I reaching York the corporation had organised a procession to visit the city's traditional proclamation points to announce the accession of the new king:
"All the gentlemen and clergy met at the Guildhall and thence to proceed to proclaim his Majesty King George the second at four different corners of the towne (viz) at the Guildhall gates the city's arms on Castlehill the pavement cross and Minster Yard stepps proceeded by the City waites-Trumpets drums and colours flying at every which places the Lord Mayor's Butler attending with the Gold Cupp his Majesty's health was drunk and after the procession ended My Lord Mayor entertained all the company at the Guildhall at the City's expense".
The four waites, including William Tireman and Charles Pick, would not have been the players of trumpets and drums there being officers of the city especially employed for that purpose. Their instruments at the time are not known but one might suspect that, as in 1739 they played oboes and bassoons.

1739   DECLARATION OF WAR WITH SPAIN

"Be it remembered that on Friday the twenty sixth day of October one

Thousand seven Hundred and thirty nine my Lord Mayor received his Majesty's writ and Declaration of War against the King of Spain and immediately ordered to be summoned the Recorder, Aldermen, and Comon Council to meet him at the Guildhall at three O'clock this afternoon....and accordingly at three O'clock in the afternoon the procession began from the Guildhall preceeded by the City Waites with their Hautboys and Bassoons and four trumpets...." Thus the council house book minuted an event very similar to the procession of 1727 and of course the participants drank heavily to his Majesty's health.

1789   THE PRINCE OF WALES AND THE DUKE OF YORK

The York Races gave the future King George IV and the young Duke their reason to visit York. After race day York put on a procession to lead the Prince to the Deanery where he received the freedom of the city. Naturally the waites led the company and later provided the music for the evening ball (presumably at the Assembly rooms). In particular they played a new Polonaise specially composed for the occasion by John Camidge, danced by the Prince and the Lady Mayoress. The prince found that he was constantly whistling the tune during the journey home and caused a letter to be written to the Lord Mayor expressing his gratitude for his hospitality in York and his delight in this new tune. Camidge gladly forwarded a copy of the work to the prince who gave it to the Band of Guards, now entitled "The Duke of York's March".

THE SHERIFFS' RIDING

For many centuries it was the Sheriffs' task to ride the city bounds, generally one week after Martinmas, the 11th of November. The mounted Sheriffs would proclaim a Christmas amnesty to beggars, whores, dice-players and others not normally welcome in York. After the riding there was a grand entertainment at the Mansion House described by William Cochrane thus in 1781:

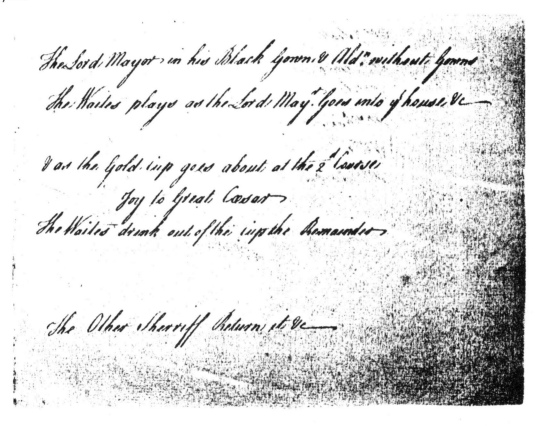

James Watson was then the leader of the five waites.

1802   PEACE PROCLAIMED

On the occasion of the proclamation of peace the waites did not lead the procession as usual but formed part of the band of the Volunteer Infantry band. They were in fact dressed in the uniform of the corps and when the proclamation had been read at each station the town clerk concluded with a cry of "God save the King" followed by three huzzas and "....the Music played that popular air". The form of the procession was given as follows:

Trumpeters
Cavalry with their Standard
Military Band
Infantry with their Colours and Streamers
Bearers of the Sheriffs' Truncheons in Scarlet
Gaoler
Officers at Mace
Under Sheriff
Town Clerk and Chaplains Sheriffs
Sword and Mace Bearers
Lord Mayor & City Council
Aldermen Gentlemen of the 24 and Common Council two and two
Free Masons two and two
(The whole flanked on either side by the Constables with their Staves)

1819   THE SHERIFFS' RIDING REVIVED

Barnard Smith and Cooke Taylor, described by The Yorkshire Gazette (Sat., Nov. 27, 1819) as "....our present spirited Sheriffs...." decided to revive their riding, a practice which had fallen into disuse only 17 years previously. They assembled their friends at Mr Wisker's in Spurriergate and partook of "a cold collation and burnt wine" before setting off to visit some seven stations to promulgate their traditional proclamation. Their retinue was huge and described as follows:

"....part of the band of the 4th Royals, next the city waits in their scarlet uniforms, one of them wearing a tattered rag cap, a badge (says Drake) of so great antiquity that the rise or origin of it cannot be found out; (presumably descended from the "old red hoode Iagged" made by John Wayte's wife in 1539) then the sheriffs, dressed in black gowns, with each a wand of office and a servant to lead his horse, with another carrying a golden truncheon, festooned with orange ribbons. Then the Under Sheriff, Mr Heron, and the Prothonotary of the Sheriffs' court, and other attendants. These were followed by nearly 200 citizens, and 70 of their sons all on horseback, and most of them wearing orange favours".

All were well-entertained after the city's generous fashion, apparently an activity very popular with Smith and Taylor whose other major claim to fame was their petition to the council earlier that month that they "....might be allowed to give the usual entertainments at the Black Swan Hotel...." events at which the waites were contracted to play. The waites fortunate enough to take part in the Sheriffs' binges in 1819 were five in number and included James Watson, Richard Brown, and Christopher Brown.

APPENDIX IV

The number of waites

The York corporation house books and chamberlains' accounts frequently supply enough detail for the number of waites in a given year to be known or calculated. Where a complete list of names or the number are not actually quoted the number may be determined by comparison of wages, or livery cloth length and cost, with years when the number is given. It has been possible to plot number of waites against time in near completeness from 1433-1836.

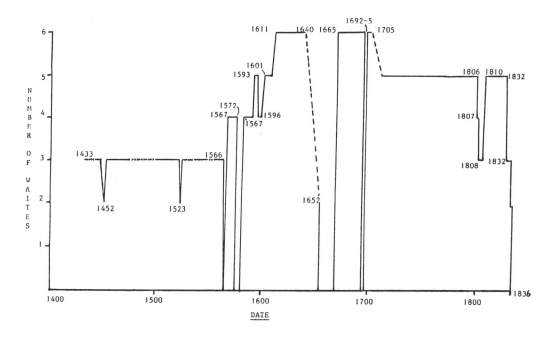

Causes of significant change in number were as follows:

1452   three to two, implied by a temporary one third reduction of cloth bought.

1523   three to two, number given.

1566-7   three to four. The three waites were sacked in 1566. In 1567 Robert Hewet was ordered to reform the band with four members.

1572   the waites were again sacked and do not reappear in the records until 1576.

1592   four-five, the five are named.

1596   five-four, on the dismissal of the elderly, deaf, drunkard, John Clerke.

1601   four-five, the five are named.

1611   five-six, six liveries stated.

1612   seven at Londesborough Hall.

ca 1650 the number of waites was run down during the civil war and in 1652 John Girdler and his sons (only J G was being paid at this time) were relieved of their posts in view of the extreme poverty of the city. Girdler petitioned to be reinstated and in 1657 was (on paper) given back his job. In 1660 the council decided that there should from then be six waites, but little happened. Girdler died in 1666, but in late 1665, probably while he was ailing, the band was reformed with six totally new players.

1692   all sacked again.

1695   six waites again in employment, implied by livery cost.

1705-27 an unevidenced decline from six to four.

1770   four-five by order of the council.

1806-33 fluctuations from five to three implied by changes in salary and caused by aging and deaths.

1833-36 in the last three years before the Municipal Corporations Reform Act the three waites are named.

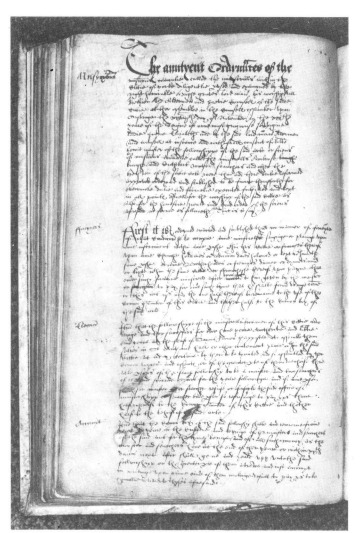

APPENDIX V

THE AUNCYENT ORDYNANCES OF THE Musicions comonlie called the Minstrills within the Cittie of Yorke diligentlie perused and examyned by the right honorable Hughe Graves lord maiour his worshipfull brethren the Aldermen and previe counsell of the saide Cittie at ther assemblee in the Counsell chambre upon Ousbrige the 28th day of November in the 21st yeare of the reigne of oure most graciouse soveraigne ladie quene Elizabeth **1578** and by the saide lord maiour Aldermen and counsell at instance and with full consent of Robt Hewitt maister of the fellowshippe af the said arte or sciens of musicions comonlie called the minstrells Ambrose Burghe and Cuthbert Watson searchers and other the brethren of the same arte were than and there dulie reformed approved ordeyned and stablished to be frome thensforth for evermore dulie and firmelie executed fulfilled and kept at all pointes aswell for the worshippe of the said Cittie as also for the honestie weale and good order of the sciens aforesaid in forme as followeth. That is to say:-

fforeyners
ffirst it is ordeyned enacted and stablished that no manner of foreyner of what Condicion he be occupie anie minstrelsse singinge or playinge upon anie instument within anie parishe within this Cittie enfranches thereof upon anie Churche holidaies or dedicacion daies holowed or kept within the same parishe or anie Brotherheades or fremans dinners or dynners mad or kepte within the same Cittie or ffranchesse thereof upon payne that everie such foraigne minstrell after moninge (admonition) to him geven by the maister or searchers to paye for everie such tyme that he shalbe found doinge contrarie to this act 3s:4d the one half thereof to remaine to the use of the Comon chamber of this Cittie and thother half to the Comon box of the said arte.

Eleccion
Item, that the fellowshippe of the minstrells freemen of this Cittie now beinge and ther successors for ever have poore Authoritie and libertie everie yeare at the feast of Saynct Iames thappostle to assemble them selves in St Anthonie hall or other convenient place within the said Cittie at a day Certaine by them to be lymited And so assembled by ther Comon voyces and assentes or the greater parte of them doe choise thre able persons of the same fellowship to be a maister and two searchers af the said science or arte for the year followinge and if anie person so chosen maister or searcher refuse or forfeyte thesaid offices of maistershipp or searcher everie person so refusinge to pay 20s thone half wherof to the Comon chamber of the Cittie and thother half to the behoof

of the said arte.

Accompt

Item, that the Comon box of the said fellowship shalbe and remaine from yeare to yeare in the custodie and keepinge of the maister and searchers of the said art for the tyme beinge and of all such money as the maister and searchers have at the end of ther year or within 20 days next after shall geve and yield upp unto the the said fellowshipp or the greater parte of them a trewe and iust accompt in writinge upon paine everie one of them makinge default to pay 10s to be equallie devided to those aforesaid.

Quarterage

Item, that everie brother of the said sciens shall pay yearlie towardes the cherge of the said art as brotherhead money 8d by yeare that is to say 2d everie quarter and that everie such ffreman beinge a brother of the said art not payenge the said quarterage everie quarter day that is to say thend of everie quarter of the yeare or within 15 daies next and immediatlie followinge after anie of the said quarter days and refusinge to content the same to pay for everie default 3s:4d to be equallie devided in forme aforesaide.

Presentacion

Item, that everie freman or brother of the saide arte present everie of his apprentices to the maister and searchers of the said arte for the tyme beinge within the one moneth ymediatlie after that anie apprentice shalbe bounde payinge at this presentacion to the Comon box of the said art 20d and if anie of them be negligent and doe not present his apprentice within the said moneth nor to pay the said fyne of 20d everie such brother so offendinge to forfaite for everie default 20s thone half to the Chamber of this Cittie and thother half to the Comon box of the said arte.

Assembles

Item, that if anie person enfranchessed to the said art or brother of the same warned by anie of the said searchers for the tyme beinge to come to the quarter daies or to thassemble of the maister and searchers of the said art for the tyme beinge with this the brethren of the same art and without reasonable cauese absenting himself not willing to come thether to pay for everie defalt 2s to be equallie devided to the uses aforesaid.

Misdemeanoures

Item, that no person enfranchised in the same art or brother of the same presume to rebuke revile or geve anie slaunderous or velenouse wordes to the said maister or searchers or to anie of them for the tyme beinge or to anie other person beinge brother or freeman of the said fellowship or art upon payne to pay for everie tyme that anie of them shalbe found culpable of anie such approbriouse or unfitting wordes to pay for everie defalt 6s:8d thone half therof to be to the Comon chamber and thother half to the Comon box of the said arte.

Teachinge

Item, that none of the said fellowship beinge a minstrell enfranchessed and brother of the said art teach or enforme anie other persons other than his owen appeentice in anie point or feat of minstrelsie except he be a fremans sone of the same arte nor goe with anie stranger to anie weddinge or anie other feast onelie to laboure with him within the said Cittie or liberties of the same without license of the maister of the said arte for the tyme beinge first obteyned upon paine to forfeyt for everie defalt 6s:8d to be devided and employed as is aforesaid Provided that this act doe not extend to anie brother for teachinge anie freman or gentleman of this Cittie and ther childrin disposed to learne anie thing for his pleasure.

Apprentishipp

Item, that no freman of the said art taike anie servant by Covenant for a yeare or otherwise oneles he be apprentice for the terme of 7 yeares at least accordinge to the lawdable custome of this Cittie upon paine to forfeyt for everie offence 20s thone half therof to be to the Comon chamber of this Cittie and thother half to the Comon box of the said arte Provided that this act doe not extend to the waites of the Cittie of York for the tyme beinge to hire anie man to helpe them in ther wache.

Secretes

Item, that no brother freman of the said art shall at anie tyme open or disclose anie wordes or sayinges lawfull touchinge ther sciens spoken at the Comon or previe meetinges of the said art or anie of them except it be to anie of the said brethren or at the tyme of ther said assemble upon paine to forfeyt for everie such defalt 6s:8d thone half therof to the use of the said chamber and the other half to the said arte.

Enhabling

Item, that no freman brother of the said art shall at anie tyme hereafter sett forth his or ther Apprentice or apprentices to laboure in anie companie as a minstrell within the said Cittie or liberties of the same before the said apprentices and everie of them be examyned and admitted by the said maister or searchers for the tyme beinge upon paine to forfeyt for everie defalt 3s:4d thone half to the chamber of the said Cittie and thother half to the Comon box of the said arte.

Teachinge of Apprentices

Item, that no brother of the said arte beinge enfranchissed shall take anie apprentice except he be able to teache him in that art both such tunynge and conversacion as he may be well thought on to serve a noble man or man of worshipp without the whoale consent of the brethren of the said art upon paine to forfeyt for everie such defalte 6s:8d thone half

to the comon chamber of
this Cittie & thother half
to the said arte.

Weddings

Item, that no brother of
the said art shall seake
for anie weddinges or
proffer himself or cawse
himself to be hired to the
same, to the hindrans of
other his brethren of the
said art except the parties
so to be married or their
friends doe send for him or
them upon paine to forfeyt
for everie such defalt
6s:8d equallie to be
devided in forme aforesaid.

Offeringe to Play

Item, that no brother of
the said art shall offer to
play in anie place within
the Cittie or suburbs where
anie of his brethren is
plainge wherebie they
shalbe worse thought of
unless he be willed or sent
for by the best man of that

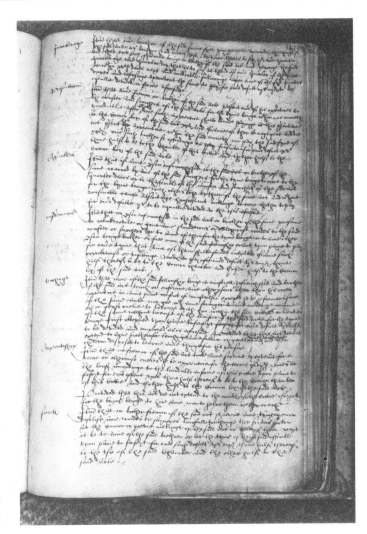

companie upon paine to
forfeyt foreverie defalt
6s:8d to the chamber & arte
aforesaid by even porcions.

Playinge at Night

Item, that no brother of
the said art beinge
enfranchessed or anie of
ther apprentices shall play
on the night before anie
mans apprentices or
servantes after nine of the
clok at night upon paine to
forfeyt for everie such
defalt 6s:8d to be equallie
paied and devided in forme
aforesaid.

Hunts Ups

Item, that no brother of
the said art enfranchessed
shall play anie huntsups at
anie tyme except the waites
of thes Cittie unlesse they
be sent for by the goodman
of the howese upon paine
to forfeyt for everie such
defalt 6s:8d equallie to be
paied and devided as is
aforesaid.

Admittance
Item, that no person shall from hensforth be made a free brother of the said art except he be examyned by the maister and whole fellowship aforesaid and be well thought on by them to be a fitt man for that purpose upon paine to forfeyt for everie such defalt 6s:8d to be paied and devided in forme aforesaid.

Pageante
Fynallie it is further ordeyned and by consent of the good men of the said art or Sciens fullie agreed that the said fellowship of minstrells of ther proper cherges shall yearelie frome hensforth when the play shalbe played bringe furth and cawese to be plaied the pagiant of corpus christi viz the Harowld his sone two counsellours and the messinger enquiringe the thre kinges of the childe Iesu sometyme accostomed to be brought forth at cherges of the lait masons of this Cittie on corpus christi day in such lyke semelie wise & order as ther occupations of this Cittie doe there pagiantes.

APPENDIX VI

Towns and cities with recorded waites

A list after Woodfill[61] and Langwill[29] with additions.
(The list must be even longer)

Aberdeen	Dartford	Lanark
Alnwick	Daventry	Lancaster
Ashbourne	Derby	Leeds
Barnstaple	Doncaster	Leeke
Barton-upon-Humber	Dublin	Leicester
Bath	Durham	Lichfield
Berwick-upon Tweed	Dover	Lincoln
Beverley	Edinburgh	Linlithgow
Bewley	Elland	Liverpool
Blyth	Exeter	London
Boston	Gloucester	Blackfriars
Bristol	Grantham	Finsbury
Bury St Edmunds	Haddington	Southwark
Burton-on-Trent	Halifax	St Giles
Cambridge	Hereford	Tower Hamlets
Canterbury	Hexham	Westminster
Carlisle	Huntingdon	Loughborough
Chester	Ipswich	Louth
Chesterfield	Irvine	Maidenhead
Cockermouth	Islington	Maidstone
Colchester	Kendal	Manchester
Coventry	King's Lynn	Marlborough
Darlington	Kingston-up-Hull	Maxfield
Darneton	Kirkudbright	Midlam

Morpeth
Newark
Newcastle upon Tyne
Newmarket
North Shields
Northampton
Norwich
Nottingham
Oxford
Penrith
Pontefract
Preston
Reading
Retford
Richmond
Ripley

Ripon
Rochester
Rotherham
Salisbury
Sandwich
Scarborough
St Eedes (St Ives?)
Salford
Salisbury
Sheffield
Shrewsbury
Skipton
Southampton
Southwark
Stamford

Stockton
Stone
Sunderland
Thetford
Thirsk
Wakefield
Warrington
Welby
Westchester
Whitehaven
Wigan
Worcester
Workington
Yarmouth
York

Punch, 18th Dec. 1907

THE UP-TO-DATE WAITS.

REFERENCES AND FURTHER READING

1. Aston, Peter."The Music of York Minster." Stainer & Bell, 1972.

2. Aylmer, GE. & Cant, R. (eds). "A History of York Minster." Clarendon Press, 1977.

3. Bridge, Prof. JC. "Town Waits and their Tunes." Proceedings of the Musical Association, 54th Session Feb 21st 1928.

4. Barlow, Jeremy (ed). "The Complete Country Dance Tunes from Playford's Dancing Master (1651-ca1728)." Faber Music, 1985.

5. Beaumont, Francis. "The Knight of the Burning Pestle." Various editions:
    a) John Doebler (ed), Edward Arnold 1967.
    b) Michael Hattaway (ed), New Mermaid 1969.
    c) Sheldon P Zitner (ed), Manchester University Press 1984.

6. Chappel, William. "Popular Music of Olden Time," 1859. Dover edition, 1965.

7. Collins, Francis (ed). "Register of the freemen of the City of York from the city records: 1272-1558." The Surtees Society vol XCVI, London, 1897 (for 1896).

8. ditto - 1559-1759. The Surtees Society vol CII, London 1900 (for 1899).

9. Cooper, TP. "The Christmas Waits and Minstrels of Bygone York," 1909.

10. Crotchet, Dotted. "York Minster." The Musical Times, May 1st. 1903.

11. Davies, Robert (ed). "Register of the freemen of the City of York 1760-1835."

12. Drake, Francis. "Eboracum," 1736.

13. D'Urfey, Thomas (ed). "Wit and Mirth or Pills to Purge Melancholy." Six vols., 1719-20.

14. Gentlemans' Magazine, The, 1746.

15. Giles, W. York Corporation House Books. Manuscript transcription of vols 39-50 (1631-1835).

16. Griffiths, David. "A Catalogue of the Music Manuscripts in the York Minster Library." Pub. York Minster Library, 1981.

17. Hadland, FA. "The Waits" in Musical News, vol 49, pp. 106-7, 125-6, 149-50, 177-8, 198-200, 214-5. 1915.

18. Harland, John. "The house and farm accounts of the Shuttleworths of Gawthorpe Hall, in the county of Lancaster at Smithils & Gawthorpe from September 1582 to October 1621." The Chetham Society, XXV, XLI, XLIII, XLVI, 1856.

19. Haxby, David. York Historian vol. 2, 1978.

20. Harvey, RM. Guildhall Library, London. Pers. Comm.

21. Hill, AF. "The Waits" in The Handbook of the Worshipful Company of Musicians, 1915.

22. "Historic Mansions." Newspaper cuttings including biographies of some two hundred Yorkshire musicians, ca 1850.

23. Hudson, Richard in Sadie, S. (ed). "Folia". The New Grove Dictionary of Music and Musicians. MacMillan, 1980.

24. Index of the wills in the York Registry. Pub. The Yorkshire Archaeological Society. Also indexes in manuscript and the wills themselves at The Borthwick Institute of Historical Research, University of York.

25. Jackson, Enderby. "Origin & Promotion of Brass Band Contests" in Musical Opinion no 228, p 815, 1896.

26. Johnston, AF & Rogerson, M (eds). "Records of early English drama-YORK." 2 vols. University of Toronto Press 1979. (Includes extracts from the city council house books (1476-1642); the civic memorandum books (1327-1547, 1371-1596, 1561-1681); the Chamberlains' accounts (1396-1642) etc).

27. Kightly, Charles & Semlyen, Rachel. "Lords of the City." York City Council, 1980.

28. Knowles, JM. "York Musicians." MS in York city library, 1924.

29. Langwill, Lindesay. "The Waits, a short historical study." Music book VII, 1952.

30. Mackerness, ED. "Somewhere Further North, a history of music in Sheffield." Pub JW Northand, Sheffield, 1974.

31. Murray, Hugh. "Pedigrees of York Families" (including Camidge and Hardman). Type-script in York City Library.

32. Palliser, David. "Civic Mentality and the Environment in Tudor York."

33. Paver's marriage licences. Pub. The Yorks. Arch. Soc.

34. Publications of the Yorkshire Parish Register Society. Various dates.

35. Rastall, Richard in Sadie, Stanley (ed). "Wait". The New Grove Dictionary of Music and Musicians. MacMillan, 1980.

36. Raven, Michael (ed). "One Thousand English Country Dance Tunes." 1984.

37. Ritson, Joseph. "A Yorkshire Garland. 1788."

38. Scholes, Percy. "The Waits and The Puritans." The Musical Times, July 1934.

39. Scholes, Percy. "The Oxford Companion To Music." O.U.P.

40. Simpson, Claude M. "The British Broadside Ballad and its Music." Rutgers University Press, 1966.

41. Smith, Lucy T (ed). "The York Mystery Plays". New York, Russell and Russell, 1963.

42. Stephen, George A. "The Waits of the City of Norwich Through Three Centuries to 1790." Proceedings of the Norfolk and Norwich Archaeological Society, vol xxv, 1933.

43. Stephen, Sir Leslie and Lee, Sir Sidney. "Dictionary of National Biography." OUP, 1960.

44. Sutcliffe Smith, J. "A Musical Pilgrimage in Yorkshire." Undated, perhaps ca 1925.

45. The Oxford English Dictionary. "Wait". Oxford University Press.

46. The York Courant, no 3155, Tues. Sept 1, 1789.

47. The Yorkshhire Evening Press, Mon. May 11, 1959.

48. The Yorkshire Gazette, Sat. Nov 27, 1819.

49.   "   Sat. Sept 15, 1832.

50.   "   Sat. July 4, 1835.

51.   "   Sat. Mar 27, 1847.

52.   "   Sat. Feb 5, 1876.

53. Travers, A. The Royal Commission on Historical Documents. Pers. comm. 1986.

54. Turner, J Horsfall. "A Yorkshire Anthology." 1901.

55. Wainwright, Jonathan P. Organist of Great St Mary's Church, Cambridge. Pers. comm. 1986.

56. Ward, John M. "The Hunt's Up." (Source misplaced).

57. White, Eileen. "The tenements at the Common Hall Gates 1550-1725." York Historian vol. 6, 1985.

58. White, Eileen. "Waits and Musicians In York 1554-1661. Entries not included in REED:York." Pers. Comm., 1986.

59. White, Eileen. "Hewet, The Wait of York." In preparation for publication, 1986.

60. Wilshere, Jonathan EO. "Leicester Town Waits." Leicester Research Services, 1970.

61. Woodfill, Walter L. "Musicians in English Society." Da Capo Presss, New York, 1969

62. York Assembly Rooms, minutes and accounts 1730-1836. York city archives.

63. York City Chamberlains' accounts. York City Archives.

64. York Georgian Society (pub). "The History of the York Musical Society and York Choral Society," ca 1948.

Illustrations were obtained from numerous sources and the Author wishes to acknowledge the following:

Iain Duncan front cover
Simon Laycock pp 18,19,20,48,53,56,59, and rear cover
John Clarke pp 4,19,64,67,69,71,74,90
Steve Thompson pp 27,86,89
Becky Nicholson p 75
Punch pp 9,131,139,175
The Illustrated London News pp 11,114
The Borthwick Institute For Historical Research pp 15,95
Julian Goodacre p 22
Jon Swayne p 23
Dover Books pp 23,25,111,116,118,126,135
York Minster Library p 35
York City Library pp 41,68,125,127
York City Archives pp 43,166,171,172
Early Music pp 92,96,104,
St Mary's Church, Beverley p 141
Musical Times p 115
Julian Drake (original drawing) p 96
Chethams Library, Manchester p 33